VERYMUCHWOW

VERYMUCHWOW
WWW.VERYMUCHWOW.COM
BIRDIE JAWORSKI
EDITOR

Donations help keep VERY MUCH WOW alive!

Our Dogecoin Address is:
DQmDQT2GoqVZmXb18w27HS6oZecpf9p3Sa

All contributors, columnists, and artists
are paid in Dogecoin
for their submissions to VERY MUCH WOW.

Want to write for VMW?
Have art to share with VMW's audience?

Please contact:
editor@verymuchwow.com

ARTWORK CREDITS

All artwork in Very Much Wow is created
by the artists credited beneath each piece.
Other pieces are copyright Very Much Wow.

SHIBES LOVE FEEDBACK

info@verymuchwow.com

Published by:

VERY MUCH WOW
Albuquerque, New Mexico, USA
T 505 216 6187

THE EDITOR

The moon watches us, creates our tides, rules our moods. The curved, feminine sphere offers a balance to the frantic angles of our world. Right now I sit at at computer whose brain is a collection of sharp pieces, connected by way of right angle or parallel surface.

The world of technology can be difficult for women to explore, even women with a strong aptitude and desire. I am older than many of the users on the community's subreddit, and I have had experiences that speak of the gender disparity in technology.

When I was a young girl in school, I wanted to take a computer programming class when our school first received several personal computers. The principal told me that I could not take the class; I was to sign up for Home Economics. You may gasp at this, but it wasn't that long ago that women, like myself, were simply not encouraged or even allowed to participate in simple technology education.

I tried to fight for the right to

The moon belongs to each of us, man and woman alike. I hope to see more Dogecoin community members encourage women and young girls getting involved in the currency. We have strong women in Dogecoin now, but imagine what our community will be like, and what it can do, if the numbers were more evenly stacked?

take the class but the principal did not budge. I learned how to bake a lemon cake why several of the boys sat at the machines and learned simple code. It has taken me all of these years to begin to explore coding, and to feel confident that I am able to excel at it.

Our own Dogecoin community has experienced several difficult conversations where questions about language - *she wants the 'D'* - ask us to examine whether the currency is stacked against half of the population. There are no solid demographic numbers for any cryptocurrency. The nature of the beast is that it is hidden in the open. The Blockchain holds no gender identity. Yet our forums and opportunities do.

I challenge our community to consider taking on a few women-friendly projects. NASCAR certainly has female fans, but the majority of interested parties are male. We have been promoting sports teams and benefiting from that exposure. Why not choose a project that benefits a strong woman, even a female athlete in keeping with the sports theme? This would open our community to the half of the population said to be ruled by our very goal: The Moon.

Birdie

SO TABLE MUCH CONTENTS

FEATURES

MUCH SCIENCE

COMMUNITY

CLAY MICHAEL GILLESPIE

Clay is an amateur writer of novels, short stories, poems and comic book scripts. His focus is on public relations. He has created and implemented strategic plans for Goodwill Industries of Central Indiana, Asian American Alliance of Indiana, Martin Luther King Jr. Dream Team, Digital Publishing Studios and Ball State University's Unified Student Media.

clay@verymuchwow.com

EDGAR BOUNDS

Edgar once bought $10 dollar time-travel voucher service that claimed to deposit $9 of the $10 dollars in a fund to accumulate over the millennia, turning into a fortune that will be used when time-travel becomes viable to go back in time and rescue him. In retrospect this may have been somewhat of an ill-conceived purchase, though he did get a rush.

edgar@verymuchwow.com

JYRO BLADE

Jyro is a video game programmer working in the New York City indie game development scene. He has been making games since he was 14 and some of his first memories involve playing Tetris on a classic GameBoy. He became involved with Doge in February 2014. Jyro enjoys DJing UK hardcore, skateboarding, and playing competitive
Magic: The Gathering.

jyro@verymuchwow.com

GOOD SHIBE

GoodShibe is a passionate advocate for Dogecoin, a regular contributor to the /r/Dogecoin community and writer of the popular 'Of Wolves and Weasels' series – an archive of which can be found at goodshibe.com.

goodshibe@verymuchwow.com

DR. LOW DOG

THEORY
DR. LOW DOG

Dr. Anthony Low is a physicist and theorist. He was born, raised and currently resides in New York City. His passion for dogs, technology, community development, and cultural disruption are confluent in his unbridled enthusiasm for Dogecoin.
lowdogtheory@verymuchwow.com

TOM

BOICE

TOM BOICE

Tom Boice is a regular contributor to the cryptocurrency news service CryptoCoinsNews.com, spearheading their weekly Dogecoin addition. Holding a B.A. in English Literature from the University of West Florida, Tom has a passion for all things music and loves analyzing song composition. He currently lives in Pensacola, FL with his wife and enjoys helping out Sean's Outpost when possible.

tom@verymuchwow.com

BARNABY GALLAGHER

BARNABY
GALLAGHER

The son of Gallagher the watermelon smashing comedian, Barnaby is best known as /u/TeaDoge; owner of a humble shop named the Tea Dojo. Barnaby works as a writer, photographer, graphic designer, and professional Sitarist. He believes in the revolutionary change Shibe spirit can cause in the world.
barnaby@verymuchwow.com

VERY MUCH DOCTOR BOB

Very Much Doctor Bob, Professor of Shibemetrics, analyzes the Dogecoin community from a variety of interesting and doge-like angles.

verymuchdoctorbob@verymuchwow.com

VERYMUCH
DOCTOR BOB

CARLISHIO2

ART SHIBE
CARLISHIO2

Carlishio2 is a coder aspiring to become a comic book artist. He lives in Puerto Vallarta. Not too long ago he had an idea for a comic based on Dogecoin. You can find his work at dogecoinball.com
carlishio2@verymuchwow.com

MANY WORDS SUCH INFO

A Very Shallow "Semantic Analysis" of "What is Dogecoin?" Video

By "Very Much Doctor" Bob

Vice President for Shibemetrics
Such Institute of Wow

Dogecoin.com published a promotional video this week, titled "What is Dogecoin." The video is also availalble at YouTube, with captioning and other info: **http://youtu.be/_KVZmS_UO5I** *(See end of report for more information.)*
The **Such Institute** conducted an analysis of the transcript. See Figure 1.

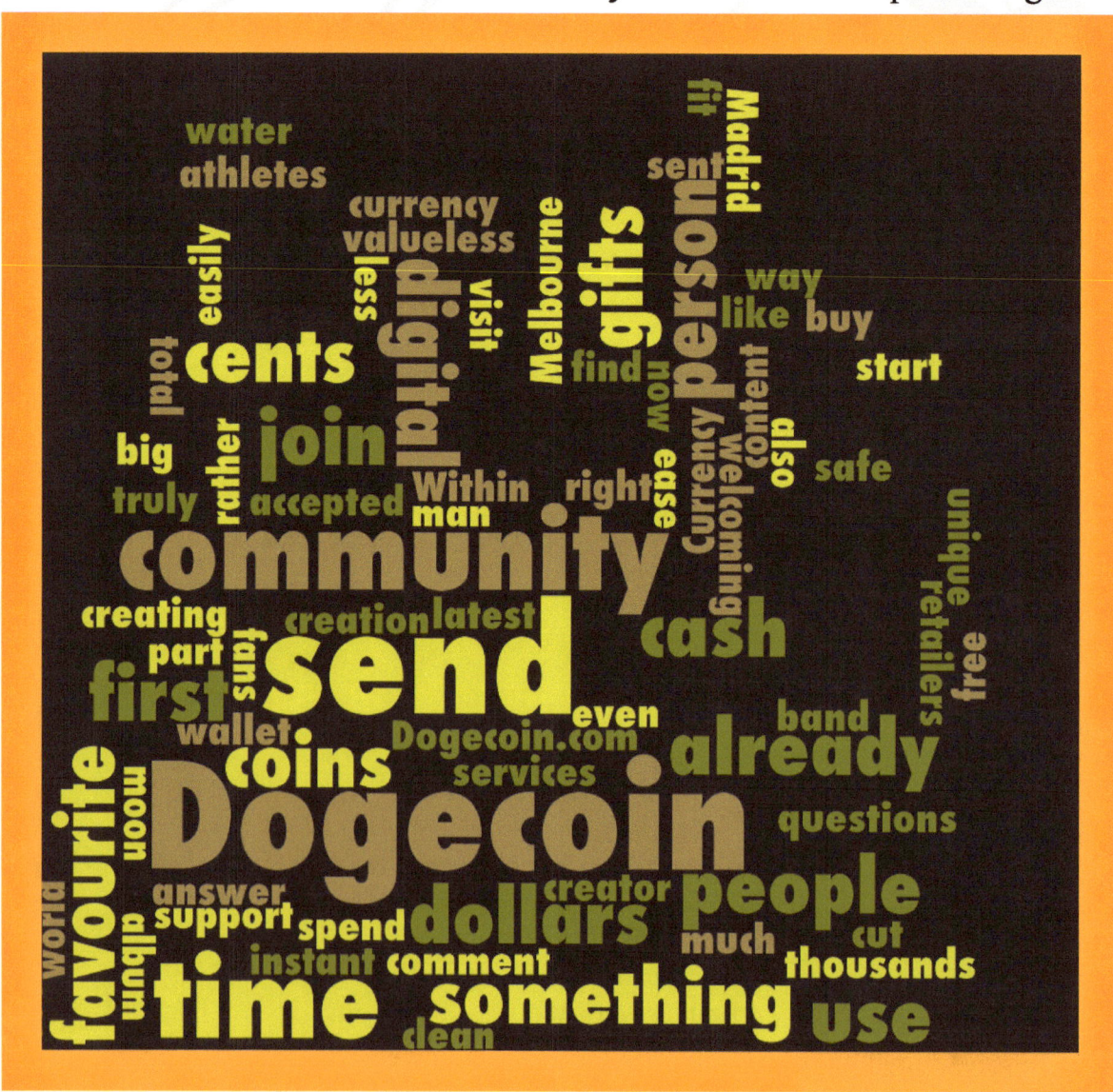

Figure 1. Much Tag Cloud: Words from "What is Dogecoin?"

VERYMUCH**DOCTOR**BOB

This figure shows the most frequent words in the video transcript, with the text size is proportional to frequency. Looking at the diagram, we see some expected words (Dogecoin, etc). But there are a bunch of words that stand out as unusual, at least in the context of cryptocurrencies. See the table.

Table 1. Frequent Words

Send
Time
Community
People/Person
Gifts

So we see that this video talks a lot about community and people, who seem to send gifts. I note that "send" ranks much higher than "receive."

Wow! Very Much Science!

About the video (from http://youtu.be/_KVZmS_UO5I)
Published on Apr 26, 2014
•**What is Dogecoin?** This video provides a simple explanation to the revolutionary currency taking the internet by storm.
•Visit http://www.Dogecoin.com to get started,
then join us at http://www.Reddit.com/r/Dogecoin
•Thanks to Robert Booth for allowing me to use his track - The Piano Sessions//
Unsquare Dance (Dave Brubeck cover) - for the video.
Check out his website here - http://robertwbooth.co.uk/
•Here's a link to the voice artist - http://voice123.com/mitchellpierson.
He is extremely professional, if you need any voice over work,
he's a great employee!

Tip
Very Much Doctor Bob ->

DRAhz9heD2SVmtZB5D2WgHwmvxudz7kLzk

LOW**DOG**THEORY

"The face of the generation will have the face of a dog."
Talmud, Sotah 49b

A cynocephalus
Nuremberg Chronicle (1493)

Russian icon of Saint Christopher

The visual culture of Dogecoin is replete with dog-headed men. There is Josh Wise, Scrooge McDuck, Snoop Dogg, astronauts, miners, Wall St businessmen, Santa Claus, even Lenin, all with the head of a doge. This is more than mere memery, this imagery has a long history and runs deep into our collective psyche.

Cynocephalus

The dog-headed man is known as the cynocephalus. The etymology has *cyno* coming from the Greek, κύων, for dog and *cephalic* coming from Latin, cephalicus, for head. The ancient Greek historians Ctesias, Megasthenes and Herodotus reported cynocephali in India and Libya. In the chronicles of his travels Marco Polo reported dog-headed men in Pakistan and in the Bay of Bengal on the island of Angamanian. The Egyptians, Chinese, Serbians, Croatians, Slavs, Saxons, Normans, Germans, Scotts and Arabs all have their own mythologies of cynocephali. It seems to be a universal theme in the human imagination. While most of the aforementioned mythologies describe these canine chimera as primitive and ferocious beings a few regard the cynocephali as religious icons.

Saint Christopher

There are many versions of the legend of St. Christopher but the most popular tell the story of a bad-ass scary face 7 1/2 foot tall Canaanite named Reprobus who wished to serve the most powerful master in the world. Reprobus began as a servant of the king of Canaan but after hearing the king feared the devil Reprobus set out to find and serve this even more powerful master. After finding and serving the devil Reprobus discovered the devil feared someone even tougher, Jesus Christ, so he set out again to find this even more powerful master. His journey led him to a Christian hermit who decided Reprobus could use his size and strength for good and help travelers cross a treacherous river nearby. Reprobus's conversion to Christopher took place upon carrying the incarnation of the baby Jesus across the river.

Though the baby Jesus was heavy, Christopher found his inspiration and powered through and completed his transformation to a bad-ass for good. Christopher was later martyred by beheading in the city of Lycia where he refused hot women and great riches and kept faith in his mission for good.

Weighing of the Heart by Anubis / Book of the Dead

In the Eastern Orthodox tradition St. Christopher is represented as having the head of a dog. This iconography clearly shows him as a very good dog.

Anubis

On deeper art historical investigations the legend of St. Christopher's is clearly related to the iconography of the Egyptian god Anubis, whom we might term the OC, original cynocephalus. Anubis, the dog or jackal headed god of Egyptian mythology was associated with the process of mummification and protection of the dead. According to ancient Egyptian religious belief, after dying one would cross the river Styx to arrive in Duat, the underworld. Here, in the Hall of Two Truths, Anubis would weigh the heart of the deceased as a final judgement. If one's heart was heavier than the feather of Ma'at, the symbol of truth, Anubis would deem you unworthy of immortality and throw you into a lake of fire to be devoured by the crocodile headed demon Ammit. Ouch, that is rough stuff. In Egyptian hieroglyphic art Anubis is often depicted beneath the scales of judgement.

Exegesis

So what are we to make of all this? What are the poetics of all these canine cabezas. What can we take from this historical imagery? Why do we seem to be rehashing these images in the visual culture of the internets? Why does it speak to us now, amidst late-capitalism, the computer age and the genesis of cryptocurrency.

The answer is to to my left. It is the face of the dog, my dog, who does not understand or care why I am tapping away at the computer and fixating on proof-of-work, the Byzantine general's problem and the birth of blockchain technologies. She wants to go out, to be free, to be outside, play and have fun. She compels me to untether from technology and stop fixating on money.

The dog and I are deeply connected, psychically, and in so much she is in my head. By pulling me away from the computer, by deactivating my neocortex and higher language function she makes me more human and a happier person. The dog judges me. She weighs my heart. By tuning my mind to that of a dog I am decapitated and made cynocelaphic. In so doing I become a better, more generous, caring person, more human and more myself. A money that represents this ethos, a money the has the head of a dog on it, is a money I want to use and invest my energy in. This is not a new joke. It is one of the oldest jokes in the world. Wow, I love Dogecoin, being in service and having the head of a dog.

Tip Dr. Low Dog:

DRLowUsgPGKRfKZorx3mUx56kNT2ZDNtcs

ROCKET MAN

*Yes. Dogecoin prepares to travel to the actual moon.
An interview with the Rocket Man who will take
Dogecoin on its ultimate journey.*

Our Dogecoin community is obsessed with the moon. We stare at her face, wanting to visit, wanting to touch her surface. She glances back at us with her best face forward, part of her profile forever hidden in darkness.

The moon holds layers of meaning: the value of our coin, the sense of community we share, and the idea that we are embarking on a journey of science and exploration. Dogecoin may just be a silly dog on a coin, but it has given many of us reasons and excuses to wonder about the worlds around and beyond us.

Team Phoenicia CEO, William Baird, knows what it's like to yearn for space. He grew up in New Mexico, land of science, ancient culture, and alleged aliens. His first job, while he was a high school student, involved working with astronomers studying potential exoplanets around pulsars.

"I went to college and earned my degree in physics," he explains. "I worked for different professors and a few small defense contractors. In New Mexico, you have the opportunity to taste different possible careers instead of being stuck in a particular path. I worked on control systems, war simulations - all of the fun stuff."

Baird laughs as he describes his stint at White Sands Missile Range.

"I got to play with overgrown Star Wars toys. We actually blew things out of the sky with giant flashlights."

Baird eventually started his own company, an internet provider in Las Cruces, New Mexico, which gave him a taste of everything good and bad in business. The business failed, but not without providing important life lessons.

"At age 20, that was a good experience," he says. "It soured me for a while, but later on I realized how much I learned and it helped me grow more successful ventures."

Baird spent three years in a highly stressful job located an hour from Las Cruces. His workday started before sunrise, and with

an office located many stories underground, he spent months of the year without seeing sunlight.

"I was losing my mind. The lack of sun made my life miserable. I was enjoying the science but I needed the connection with the real world. Then I took a job at Lawrence Berkeley Lab. I worked on supercomputers, 15 million dollar machines," he reminisces.

It was here that Baird first started thinking about space travel.

"Around 2007, I started working on the Google X Prize competition. We didn't become an official team until 2010," he says. "We figured out the technical side of it; we could build a rocket and a lander. Those things are very involved in a scientific sense, but they aren't difficult in the overall scheme of things."

What Baird didn't anticipate was what it takes handle the actual rocket launch.

"The launch itself is a whole 'nother beast, and is almost bigger than the rest of the journey," he sighs. "There is so much paperwork, and so many little things you must provide. You don't just give your specifications to Lockheed. It's much more complicated than that. So, we decided that with the cost of launches being as high as they are, we would find someone else who is already flying. If they could take

our payload, we could launch from orbit and head to the moon."

Every single primary payload provider - such as satellite companies - said, "No." Baird's technology was solid, the companies relayed to him, but the proposition made no business sense on account of the risk it would add to the launch.

"One of the VPs broke it down in financial terms," Baird explains. "These projects have such a slim margin of profit. Even though each component may cost billions of dollars, you will end up earning just a few million bucks for your years of time, effort, and assumption of risk. Even adding a half-of-a-percent addition risk factor in taking our payload was not worth it for any of these companies. For them, it was just a business decision, but for us, it was our work and our life."

Baird and his team realized that they needed to control the launch themselves if they were ever going to make it to the moon.

"The launch requires a small army to deal with the paperwork," he describes. "We learned what was involved, and started partnering with different organizations and companies to make it happen. We decided to turn this into a business that allows other riskier payloads - like ours - as well as others who can't afford to get onto primary launches to make it into space.

We started a fractional payload service."

Baird discovered cryptocurrency during his rocket launch development.

"My interest actually came out of a joke here at work. We were facing the big government shutdown threat last year, and we all joked that we should turn our supercomputers into Bitcoin mining devices. We have two of the fastest computers in the world, and laughed that we could make up the budget using them."

Baird started researching cryptocurrency and was shocked to discover that his expensive state-of-the-art machines were not the best kind of computer for mining cryptos; rather simple ASICs devices which used small amounts of energy and devoted their entire existence to performing on function excelled.

"It blew my mind," he says. "I started digging around and found Ry Buscoe and his company, RevUp Render. We started talking about Dogecoin. Ry told me that the community wanted to go to the moon. Why not make it really happen?"

Baird and Buscoe discussed ways to get Dogecoin to the moon and developed the idea of a Lunar Iditarod - a race of cellphone-sized micro rovers on the moon.

"The joke and the seriousness of it all fell into place," Baird laughs. "We bounced it off a few people including Dogecoin founder Jackson Palmer. Now it's official. We are going to the moon and we are taking Dogecoin."

VeryCharity, Inc., the first fully incorporated entity created for the sole purpose of promoting Dogecoin, is the crypto's interface with the space team. The organization is helping to provide a framework for Dogecoin community involvement in the project.

The competition involves a series of stages on the ground between self-organized teams. Some universities are already organizing teams for the competition. The micro rovers are called "Dogesleds," in honor of the famous dogsled race. Each rover will be be 3 centimeters tall, 5 centimeters wide, and 10 centimeters long when stowed, weighing no more than 85 grams. They will each have a RevUp Render logo as well as a Dogecoin logo, in addition to a 1 megapixel camera.

The stages pit teams against each other in a series of head-to-head elimination races. Each team must demonstrate that their rover can meet the rigors of space travel and the inherent difficulties in the lunar surface while racing and sending back photographs for the audience on Earth.

Before the rovers can race, they have to make it to the moon. Baird has launch plans which can not yet be revealed, but will involve his rocket - filled with payloads from other Google X Prize competitors as well as the Dogesleds. The launch will send the rocket to a geosynchronous polar orbit.

"After that, the upper stage will relight and put us on a translunar trajectory," Baird says. "We will release not only the landers, but we will have some CubeSats to release as well. One of the teams flying with us will be carrying the little rovers, and once they have landed, they will send back a video stream. The rovers will also send back snapshots every ten seconds during the race. There are many steps a team must take to make a sound rover. It needs to be able to travel across the lunar regolith, which is abrasive and can clog and jam many mechanical things with ease."

Baird expects teams to come up with different kinds of rover designs, each involving distinctive methods of locomotion.

"There may be ones designed with legs, ones that rotate or slither forward like a snake. A team might utilized a spring and have their rover leap nine meters through the lunar sky," he describes. "The rovers have to fit within the allowed dimensions and have no dangling parts. They will be ejected out of the lander by a simple mechanical spring, so they need to be sturdy as well."

Baird envisions ways in which the Dogecoin community can enjoy and support the competition. He plans to hold a t-shirt design contest once the competition is underway.

"The teams will all come out of the community," Baird says. "The more we have, the better. We are open to ideas from the community about what other kinds of exciting side events we can hold during the competition."

The moon means as many things to William Baird as it does to each of us.

"It's the goal I've wanted since I first saw Star Wars as a kid," he says. "Ever since then I've been in love with space. The moon is that goal. You see the moon rise every evening. It is the ultimate monument. I will be able to point to the moon and say, 'I did that.' Anything we put up there will last a long, long time, beyond the time the pyramids turn into dust, probably beyond the time of the last human on earth. Billions of years from now, in the moments before the sun becomes a red giant and swallows the solar system, our rovers will still rest on the moon. That's as close to eternal as we can get in this lifetime."

Learn more about the Lunar Iditarod at the project website:

lunariditarod.revuprender.com/

VeryCharity, Krytos, and ShibeNet form "The Peloton"

Moving forward VeryCharity (USA) , Kryptos (a German non profit entity) and ShibeNet (Australia based) have reached an accord to share resources and to utilize the specialist knowledge in their respective areas. With this accord in place, there now exists a functional group that has the capabilities to conduct the operations of a foundation, yet with each part of the distributed group having autonomy in its activities and coming together as and when the need arises.

The accord is going under the name of "The Peloton" and other aligned entities are actively encouraged to contact one of the above named groups to discuss getting involved. Visit VeryCharity.org for information.

Expresscoin Begins Selling Dogecoin

Expresscoin.com has begun selling Dogecoin for USD. The company has been selling Bitcoin for a number of months, and has recently added Dogecoin to its offerings. Customers may purchase Dogecoin with money orders - which one can obtain at any Postal Office - or via a bank transfer. Learn more at Expresscoin.com.

v8 SuperDogeCar Project Now Accepting Donations

ShibeNet is supporting a promotion to wrap a V8 Supercar in Dogecoin imagery. The car will be driven by Lee Holdsworth of Erebus Motorsport. Interested shibes may support the v8 SuperDogeCar Project:

http://www.dogeraiser.com/c/25
DSjaTHgheXcdugKz9TZYUtXAAcNi15YD6G

Gallery Auctions Artwork in Dogecoin for Charity

Downtown L.A.'s AGIT Gallery is hosting "Experiment 87a" a celebration of the .gif. To mark the occasion, the organizers will be holding a silent auction where patrons can bid on select works using the cryptocurrency Dogecoin. All proceeds from the auction will be transferred to the Dogecoin Foundation's general charitable fund directly following the election of the organization's new board of directors.

Got News? Send your press releases to:
editor@verymuchwow.com

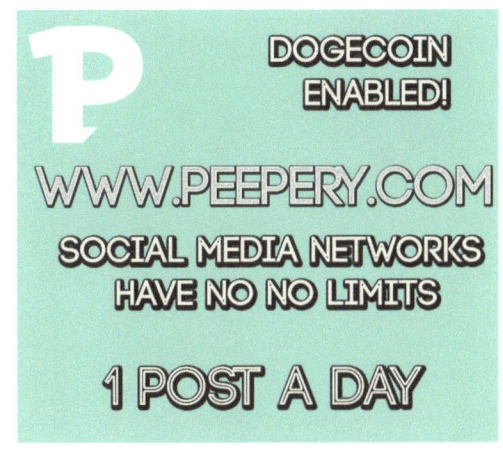

A REVIEW OF FLAPPY DOGE

When Flappy Bird, created by Nguyễn Hà Đông and published by .GEARS Studios, debuted in the summer of 2013, it went mostly unnoticed until a sudden spike in popularity in early 2014. People became obsessed virtually overnight , and it skyrocketed to the most downloaded free game on the iOS App Store by the end of January 2014. The obsession was short-lived however. Early the next month, the creator pulled the game from the store, citing guilt about the seemingly unhealthy addiction players showed for the game.

The addictive spirit of Flappy Bird lives on today in Flappy Doge, by Flappy.me, which is available to download for free on the Google Play store for Android devices. Flappy Doge is one of many clones of the original that reskins the main character and environment, but seeks to keep the original gameplay that made Flappy Bird so popular.

Players control a derpy looking Doge that automatically moves across the screen. The Doge is affected by gravity and will crash into the ground unless the player taps the screen to make the Doge fly up. The more you tap, the higher your Doge will fly. After the player avoids the ground for a bit, Super Mario-esque pipes will appear on the screen for the player to dodge. Pipes spawn from the top and bottom of the screen simultaneously, creating a small window through which the Doge must fly. For every pair of pipes successfully navigated, the player scores a coin. Play continues until the Doge collides with either the pipes or the ground. Players are then told their final coin total, which serves as their score, and possibly awarded a medallion based on performance.

The game is intentionally difficult, with many runs ending after only acquiring a small number of coins. This actually acts as the main draw of the game, as players find themselves frustrated at their loss and return to attempt a better score over and over again.

The visuals of Flappy Doge leave a bit to be desired as there are only two pixel art style backgrounds, one of which is randomly chosen at the start of each run. The original game, did not even feature a secondary background, so technically this is an upgrade. In an attempt to distance the art from the Super Mario franchise, the pipes have been reskinned to blue from the traditional green. The style of the Doge avatar itself seems like a strange choice, but apparently it was changed from an original design due to copyright issues, so perhaps some leeway can be given there.

The main negative for the game is the overall annoying sound effects. Upon tapping to make the Doge fly up, users get a feedback of what is perhaps supposed to be a dog barking, but ends up sounding more like a metallic crunching sound. As the Doge passes through a pair of pipes, the same ding sound is repeated for each coin acquired. Finally, hitting an object plays a sharp "woof" noise that is also rather unpleasant. The lack of a mute button exacerbates the audio problem, so players are forced to either turn their device audio off entirely, or hear the grating game audio

constantly.

Overall Flappy Doge is an excellent clone of the original and features what I consider to be an improved experience. I feel the developer could have easily included more art for the background or obstacles, but the addition of even a second background is still much appreciated. Flappy Doge is fantastic little timewaster, but if there is ever a game that has needed a mute button, it's this one.

Tip Jyro:
D6SbM3coVCo7uYrqJZBMPJbSb476e5AhfM

FLAPPY DOGE

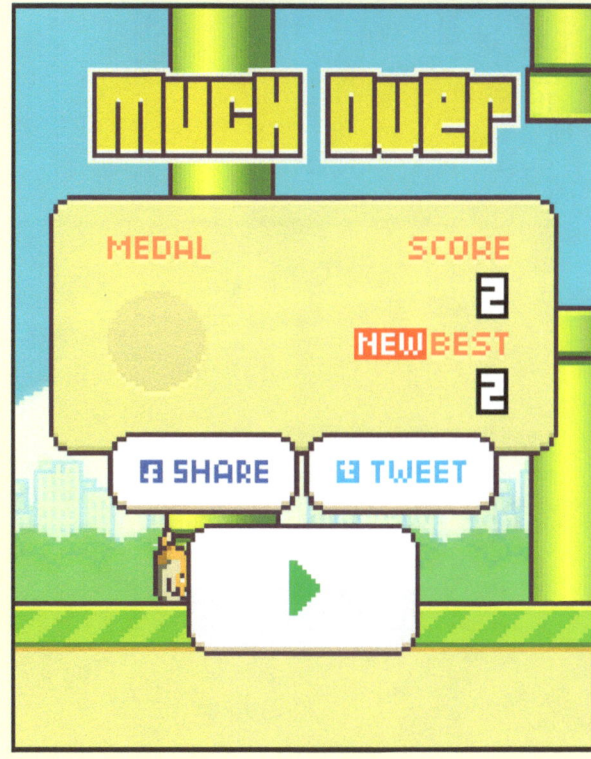

PHOTO of the MONTH

GRAFFITI DOGE BY TAKER | /U/TAKERONE ON REDDIT | TAKER.HU ON THE WEB

Tip Takerone:

DTAKERqwW2jz77GmEJK18dGqkBDAwf8Cbj

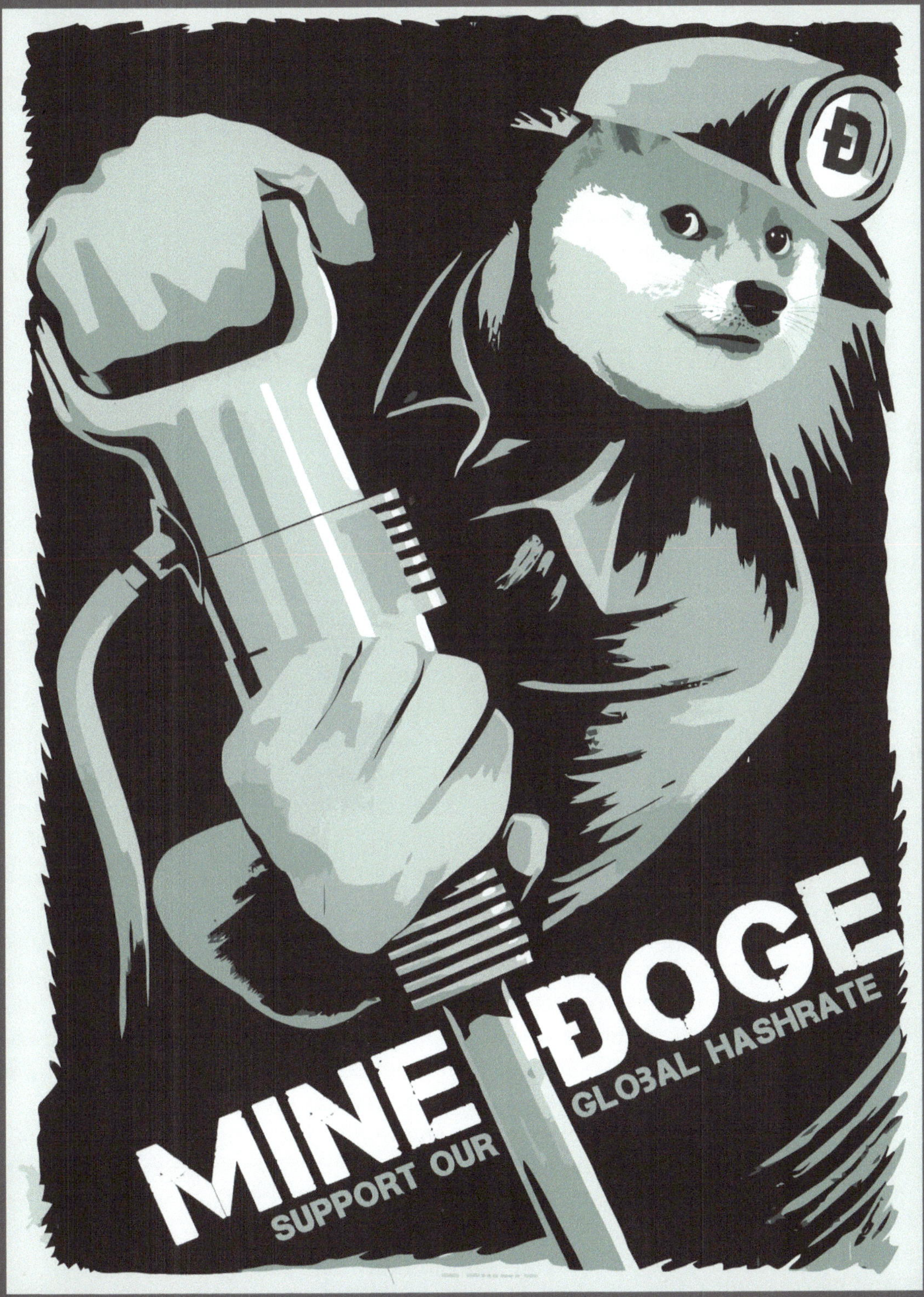

ORIGINAL ART BY /U/NEED4DOGE

Tip /u/need4doge:

D7RVX7kVw3yfK4uUYGUXx1dkiSk4rrSf9B

NEWS SHIBES

You have the Dogecoin! They have the daily news! Learn which Shibe-run News Sites are rocking the updates, and which social communities have something to offer YOU!

THE DAILY DOGE
www.dailydoge.org

News Shibe "Howard" runs The Daily Doge, an easy-to-navigtate site that features daily updates on All Things Dogecoin.

Howard's news is well-written, original, and often contains thoughtful insights on Dogecoin economy, community, and technology.

The site is separated into four sections: Dogecoin Mining, Dogecoin News, Dogecoin Guides, and Dogecoin Sites. You may click on any of these headings to find a list of recent Dogecoin news stories.

Howard isn't afraid to share other Dogecoin news sites with his readers; he regularly features reviews of Dogecoin sites of all kinds, including fellow news shibes.

Readers of The Daily Doge are invited to connect with Howard via comments on the site, through Twitter, and by singing up for a newsletter.

RECOMMENDED

FOLLOW THE COIN
followthecoin.com/dogecoin/

Follow the Coin calls itself the "Homepage of Digital Currency." The site covers Bitcoin and Dogecoin news and entertainment through the eyes of its contributors. Dogecoin reporters include Dogetipbot creator Josh Mohland and Dogecoin founder Jackson Palmer.

Primarily a video news platform, Follow the Coin creates entertaining, colorful videos that quickly cover a variety of timely topics, from gossip-type rumors hitting the /r/dogecoin subreddit to reporters on the scene of big events such as Josh Wise's recent Talladega race.

Some of Follow the Coin's news shorts have a soft, feel-good flavor, choosing to highlight community activities and discussions about why Dogecoin is good for humanity.

If you enjoy a multimedia approach to your news, Follow the Coin may be for you!

VIDEO NEWS

MUCH DOGE NEWS
www.muchdogenews.com

Much Doge News is one of the better news aggregator sites with a social networking twist. The site invites readers to submit news stories

Much Doge News also provides a handy Doge value calculator at the top of the site; of course 1 Doge will always equal 1 Doge, but it's nice to see where the crypto stands relative to other cryptos and the USD.

One thing I like about Much Doge News is that readers may give a vote to submissions that they find worthwhile, much like a Facebook "like." You may also subscribe to the site and receive regular updates.

The site's owner is active at the Dogecoin subreddit and always willing to help a new Shibe get a wallet or figure out the dogetipbot.

SOCIAL NEWS

TWITTER

Some of the most intelligent, fun, and fascinating Dogecoin happenings and discussions happen over Twitter. Shibes regularly connect to share graphic memes, Dogecoin news, event updates, and help each other crowdsource projects and charity drives.

There are more women interested in Dogecoin participating in Twitter than in any other forum or venue. Twitter offers a safe and curated space to engage in conversations with others who share interests without concern of creepy stalkers. Hey, we women have these concerns!

Twitter also offers an unprecedented opportunity to share your thoughts with big names in media, entertainment, and business. You may tweet something that a shibe said and find it retweeted by The Guardian in the UK!

Hashtags that you may find useful are:
#dogecoin
#tothemoon
#thingsshibessay

SHIBETTES!!!!

DOGECOIN SUBREDDIT
reddit.com/r/dogecoin

Is something happening in the world of Dogecoin? Who ya gonna call? /r/dogecoin, of course! The first beating heart of the Dogecoin universe, the sub has a fast-moving forum where shibes from across the world connect to complain about and praise their favorite crypto.

The Dogecoin subreddit has an astonishing 86K membership base at the time of this issue's publication. Regardless of the time of day or the year, you will be in the company of hundreds of like-minded Dogecoin holders and tippers.

Many Dogecoin enthusiasts learned about cryptocurrency through the sub, and received their first few dogecoins as a thank you for a funny or kind comment. Sometimes the sub gets a little rowdy - who can forget the Angela White escapade?

In addition, the Dogecoin community at reddit has several other subs devoted to Dogecoin news in which users post links to stories and events.

DOGE CENTRAL

DISCUSS.DOGECOIN DOT COM

The official Dogecoin Community Forums are new and not widely used - yet. But the site is wonderfully conceived, easy-to-use and offers a gentle and helpful introduction to those new to Dogecoin as well as those well-versed in All Things Doge.

The site - a subdomain of the official Dogecoin.com URL - is broken down into useful categories. You may post your artistic creations in "Art & Design," or chat with some of the smartest minds in crypto in "Development Talk."

The site offers a slower pace than the reddit sub. It also invites shibes to engage in thoughtful and considered conversation. All of your favorite Dogecoin "celebrities" have made an appearance at Discuss. Dogecoin - why not make an appearance yourself?

RECOMMENDED

BUY SOMETHING WITH DOGECOIN
EVERY DAY!

DON'T KEEP YOUR DOGE BOTTLED UP

DON'T LET OUR ROCKET CRASH. USE YOUR DOGE!

FALLEN MISSLE OUTSIDE OF WHITE SANDS MISSILE BASE / PHOTO BY BIRDIE JAWORSKI

BARNABY GALLAGHER

It is early morning, and the Hall of Frontpage is buried ankle deep in loose Dogecoins, sleeping Shibes, and the burnt fragments of countless spent UpRockets. Celebration will continue for days; Josh Wise has won the Sprint Fan vote. But my crew is already awake. We are busily loading carts, camels, and all manner of animals with goods of every kind. An All Star rises in the East. There could not be a better omen on the day of departure for the Caravan of the Doge.

My name is Barnaby, The Tea Doge. I am a Musician and Merchant. Today we leave the city ArrDogecoin, for the limitless plains of the Internet. The world can no longer deny the strength of the Shibe Heart, or the things that people united in cooperation can achieve. ArrDogecoin, how I will miss your golden walls and parapets! How grand shall you be on my return? Every day more Shibes move in, but it is time for us to move out. The heart is strong, but for the body of Dogecoin to grow... it must have veins.

"Hah" I say outloud. It was almost a snort. "Soon, every day will be May the 4th. Every day shall be "Buy something with Dogecoin day." I finish my breakfast of pineapple, watermelon, and jasmine pearl tea. Scarcely before the dishes are clean and boxed away, my tent is collapsed and skillfully tucked into the last cart. Euu MostlyRegrets approaches, slogging through the sand. This land was not a desert when ArrDogecoin was founded, but the climate soon changed due to the heat ever rising from the mines. He comes from the city gate to bid farewell, and help me fasten the giant rope and tassel on my wagon. I do not see Euu Goodshibe anywhere, but the Mail Doge scurries out to us and delivers this mornings Wolves and Weasels 129.

It is all about Josh Wise! As things should be. Winning the vote yesterday was a milestone in our history.

My victory will come more slowly, like a Camel. But thankfully, every Shibe has been carried that much closer with a roaring ride in the Dogecar. Seeing the face of Kabosu alongside financial titans such as Lowes, McDonalds, Miller, and CAT has a profound effect. It brings the gift of legitimacy.

"My Caravan is loaded with many things, but the greatest treasure we will ever bring to distant lands is our culture. A culture of inclusiveness, equality, generosity, and fun."

Time, you old gypsy man, will you not stay, put up your caravan just for one day?   - Ralph Hodgson

Legitimacy leads to Faith, and Faith leads to the only thing which will truly bring our paws to lunar soil, Acceptance. Acceptance of Dogecoin as a store of value, and form of payment. In my journey I hope to find artists, craftsmen, teachers and engineers. The people of the world. Through their good faith in accepting Dogecoin for their gifts, we move forward.

My Caravan is loaded with many things, but the greatest treasure we will ever bring to distant lands is our culture. A culture of inclusiveness, equality, generosity, and fun. A new chapter in finance, and a new face for the idea of money. An idea that many associate with limitation, instead of empowerment. For hundreds of years, humankind has given its power away; to Kings, Clergymen, Governments, or Banks. The money everyone used was backed by them. Dogecoin is backed by everyone, by the faith of each person who uses it. (It is also backed by Tea; because as long as I live, I will accept Dogecoin in exchange for it!)

Businesses of the world; I believe the technologies inherent in cryptographic currencies are an improvement over the way we do things now. But those benefits will only fully blossom with wider acceptance. The most important reason to invest in Dogecoin is because of what it means.

The spirit of a Shibe is always concerned with the well being of others, and the well being of the planet. They value compassion, and fairness, and believe that every living thing is worthy; not for what it can do or produce, but for what it is. Shibes know that in order to create a more harmonious world, it will take a lot of work. But they also know, that no one needs to break their back if everyone works together. Shibes see a future where every place can be as joyous as ArrDogecoin. They know we live in a strange and beautiful universe that is waiting to be played with and explored... if we would only stop fighting and polluting our home. If a peaceful and thriving planet has any value to you, then you must admit to the value of Dogecoin.

I bid many Shibes farewell, and climb up onto a shaded coach. The Caravan begins its journey into the unknown.

I look back at ArrDogecoin. It glows beautifully in the red light of Dawn. Euu SilentShibe stands high upon the walls, cloaked. SpeakAlwaysTheTruth stands beside him, flexing. The wallet on my belt becomes slightly heavier in an instant.

I smile, and wave Goodbye.

SpeakAlwaysTheTruth flexes,
And SilentShibe says nothing.

Tip Barnaby:
DHW3se4b52bbxochT8tNLNf3QMK1YB2qYa

BARNABY GALLAGHER

carlishio2

CARLISHIO2

Tip Carlishio2:

DJC9wryzi5SWt2Z25HdR9eHeuzcZxZJZEA

ART SHIBE

CARLISHIO2

WATCH ME REVIEW

CLAY MICHAEL GILLESPIE

Spiderman: Electrifyingly Captivating Despite Mixed Reviews

Photo courtesy of Marvel Comics and Columbia Pictures with a twist of VMW artistic manipulation

> "Jamie Foxx plays both sides of the coin in the way 'The Amazing Spiderman' series needed: dark, disturbed and something that Spiderman fans haven't seen before."

In my last review of Captain America: The Winter Soldier, I marveled at the audio production that allowed me to feel every gut-wrenching punch that Cap made on screen.

I'd like to say now that my previous judgment on the height of audio production has been completely overthrown by the electrifying destruction caused by the main villain from "The Amazing Spiderman 2", Electro.

Zapping its way onto the big screen May 2 and opening at a $92 million debut, Spidey takes on the electrifying menace Electro, played by Jamie Foxx,

in this adventure of the slightly controversial reboot in the series.

If you've ever questioned the need of proper speakers and visuals when watching a movie, wait until the first big battle between Spiderman and Electro takes place. Backed by a powerful Hans Zimmer score, Electro uses his new-found powers to the full extent multiple times, and you can feel his electrifying pulse creep through your veins as they cause absolute mayhem on screen.

It cannot be stressed enough how awe-inspiring the shocking sounds were, and how necessary they were to the progression of Electro. Even when Max Dillon is introduced, there are little hints all throughout the speakers as to how his mind works. The audio production and cinematography during the villainous scenes are incredibly captivating and entertaining, and give quite a few extra points to a film that's received mixed reviews.

The re-imagining of Electro is unique. While Max Dillon and Electro may seem like two different people in terms of character development, Jamie Foxx plays both sides of the coin in the way "The Amazing Spiderman" series needed: dark, disturbed and something that Spiderman fans haven't seen before.

Speaking to character development, Marvel has a knack for casting the absolutely best people for the job. Andrew Garfield doesn't just play Spiderman, but he's also a perfect Peter Parker. Spidey is witty, quick, funny and an emotionally disturbed wreck of a man on screen shown through his anger and believable tears. It begs the question, "why did we settle for Tobey McGuire for three films?"

Garfield really had to tap into his acting ability in this movie. He's haunted by his past along with a city that won't allow to him to be the hero he needs to be as he creates his own villains in the classic Spiderman way. Not only all of that, but Parker is in love with a beautiful woman.

At the end of the last film, we saw his rekindled love for Gwen Stacey, played by the always-wonderful Emma Stone. Now, not only does Parker have to be a masked-vigilante saving New York one crime at a time, but a lover who's heart is held in the hands of a beautifully conflicted woman. For

once, this is a love story in a comic book movie that you'll actually enjoy experiencing.

Unfortunately, while the film was entertaining to watch, it was not a perfect movie. There were quite a few plot lines that many other critics have noted needed to be simplified down. The film was not a disaster by any means, but its role for furthering the series seemed a tad forced. There are a lot of plans for the future of the Spiderman universe, but it can't be done the same way as "The Avengers".

"The Avengers" had a distinct advantage in its formulation. They had Iron Man movies, a Thor movie, a Captain America movie and even a Hulk movie before unveiling their big plan. Spiderman is only one series, and needs to take the time to develop the storyline through several movies to allow their plans to come through. The same can be said for DC's Justice League movie on the always-nearing horizon, as they do their best to cram the entire DC universe into one big upcoming film.

At least the writers do their best to capture the classic Spiderman comic-book feel to the movie. There are some incredibly cliché and campy lines throughout the movie, along with a few really stereotypical side-villains, but I wouldn't say this is a weakness. The writing team seem to be doing their very best to stay true to the story-line that Spiderman fans want, but also differentiate themselves from the previous Tobey McGuire series.

They're stuck in two conflicting states of mind. When watching the scenes with Parker and Stacey compared to the rest, it

almost seems like you're watching two different movies at times. Harry Osborne, Electro, OSCORP and others are given much deeper scenes while Parker and Stacey are surrounded by a very different aura. This may just be another side-effect of complex series-progression though, to which I am willing to overlook for the sake of enjoying the movie.

Regardless of what other reviews say, this was a good comic-book movie. A lot of what I've read doesn't pay any attention to the detail put into the film through the audio, video, and villain plot-lines. After taking these into account and noticing where the series is headed, I'd still recommend it.

I would say that this film experience is absolutely worth the money. Pay attention to the subtleties the movie offers. It's cool to see how the writers are giving villains the attention they deserve, rather than focusing solely on the hero. This is going to be a series that surprises people, and you're going to want to be a part of it.

Tip Clay:

DLJ1TcXNJShKNbK7GUxsQSovdVMz6RwaKe

The Power of People and Fast Cars

We are born into a world that is fundamentally unfair. We are shaped by our genetics, our early family life, our culture, our economic status, our access to education, our area of residence. We are each a child of a terrible toss of galactic dice. We can shift our position in society in small ways through experience and sheer tenacity. Some of us can catapult into a different sphere altogether. Nothing happens in a vacuum, however. We cannot elevate our situation in life without the help of others, of earth-bound angels.

In our daily travels, we drive past so many hungry people that we lose count. We drive past so many hungry people that our journey becomes a video game, our headlights laser guns designed to obliterate obligation. We drive past so many hungry people that we forget that we are hungry for something other than food.

Everyone has a story about the man who needed a dollar for gas, about the woman wandering the neighborhood looking for empty cans, the pregnant teenager with nowhere to turn. These are the spirits that haunt the holy books, waiting for our hardened skin to crack. Some of us - those with big enough hearts who understand life's unkind nature - will step forward, offer help.

Fulvio Gerardi is one of these people. His network of shibes ready-to-help, ShibeNet, is already changing lives across the globe. I spoke to Fulvio over Skype and asked him about ShibeNet and his new project to sponsor - with Dogecoin, of course - a V8 Supercar. Fulvio's avatar is a graphic that states "99%" in a bold typeface. This is not a man afraid of someone else's opinion, not afraid to stand with his fellow human beings.

- Birdie

How did you first learn about Dogecoin?

I've been a coin collector for quite some time and participate in coin forums. Somebody brought up the subject of Bitcoin in September of 2013. We got to talking about it, but people were generally negative about the whole thing. I investigated Bitcoin, tried to get into it. I set up a Litecoin wallet. According to what I was reading, I should have been able to mine coins with the wallet, but it didn't work. There was no community as such.

Someone poped up in the forum and said that they were getting into this Dogecoin thing.

I grabbed a wallet, and it took forever to synchronise. I found faucets, and from there on it became a bit of a progression. I could only CPU mine as I am on a Mac. Sites that I found kept pointing to Reddit.

I finally bit the bullet and joined the Dogecoin subreddit a month ago. A couple of people threw coins at me. I learned how to use the dogetipbot. You get some coins, you give some coins. I got in the habit of doing tip runs, but. I would come out with more than I put in. I learned how to transfer funds, and now I'm moving stuff back and forth between the tipbot and my wallet.

Tell us about ShibeNet and how it started.

I joined a LEO's club when I was a teen. I have a friend who is president of the Rotary Club. I've been volunteering all of my life. It's all been good fun.

Here I am in this situation where things are starting to happen. That was when Eki showed up. (*Ed. note: Eki is a beloved member of /r/dogecoin.*) I tripped over a post of his where he was asking what was wrong with his leg; I've been there and done that a year ago and advised him. People were throwing money at him - they paid for a doctor. He needed a compression. I had one from the hopsital and sent it to help. I did what I could to help him. What I found is that throwing money is really simple. The difficulty is in turning that money into things you actually need.

FULVIO GERARDI

"Enthusiasm is great, but don't be one-eyed. Give every project a little bit of love and you won't regret it."

I went looking for someone to help. I found a group of Dogecoiners in Turkey, I got in touch and they let me into the group. One of them met Eki and took him out for dinner, and the group raised the funds to get Eki a place to live. The thread about it went to number one on the Dogecoin subreddit and got Eki a nice sum of dogecoins.

We decided that we needed people on the ground, and we came up with ShibeNet. What if we had a shibe in every major city in the world? I wouldn't mind going anywhere in Melbourne to help anyone. Imagine someone in Sidney, a guy in Brisbane, a network of people that when a problem came up, there would be someone there.

We started ShibeNet 21 days ago. We started collecting people from all over the world. We have a Google map that shows the locations of every shibe in the network. We are working on putting a database into place that will allow us to immediately find and reach the closest shibe when a problems arises.

Why fund a v8 Supercar?

NASCAR has been great fun, but it is a sport with very US centric fan base. We wanted to fund something that had a more global appeal. We found a team that needed sponsorship, made a few calls, and they were enthusiastic. The NASCAR voting was

Wrap it in Doge!

Continued on next page >

happening at the same time, so our posts on this didn't get much traction at Reddit. I pulled my head in and thought about it for a little bit.

In the meantime, someone who shall remain anonymous made an offer of 10K USD for the project, and, at the same time, Cathy Keth had been posting around with the Bahay Kubo project which builds huts for homeless children in the Philippines. We kept running into each other. She had been trying to raise scholarship money for three kids, and now these kids have a roof over their head.

So I thought about how we could tie these three things together - ShibeNet, the education project, and the car, and put it all in front of people's eyeballs. We started a subreddit and invited the community to help The guy who did the wrap for Josh Wise's car is there, Josh Mohland is there. We put up a pledge thread and already more than 40 people have pledged to help.

We decided that if the V8 project doesn't come together, then the 10K pledge goes to the team to put a Dogecoin logo on the car, and we give the other donated funds to Cathy's project. If we can help her fund the project - which isn't a lot of money - it helps real kids in the world. We are sure we can raise enough funds to get the car bonnet done in Dogecoin, but we would like to fund the full car and Cathy's project.

You are involved in both promotions and charity work with Dogecoin. Is it a good fit?

I'm looking at this from a few different angles. I'm also looking at this from what accomplishments we can get for the currency.

I've done this sort of thing professionally. I know what I'm doing. I don't want to be the man in charge. I've run major corporations in various fields. I've done that kind of thing. Dogecoin is decentralized. What I do want to do is get the message across to all shibes that they can do it, too. I went from my very first dogecoin to fundraising in a couple of weeks.

Everyone who joins Dogecoin today could be on the bus by the end of the month. If every single person does something and gets one more person interested in Dogecoin, then we don't need one person to go out and find 10,000 people.

The combination of charity and promotion works. All of the good work in the world is worth nothing without promotion.

Any advice for the shibes of the world?

Enthusiasm is great, but don't be one-eyed. If you are so wildly enthusiastic about one project, and something bad happens, it leaves you with nothing. Give every project a little bit of love and you won't regret it.

Take Eki, for example. Even at his worst he was tipping people, helping people, and I think not a lot of people are like that. A lot of people disappear up their navels and say, "Oh woe is me." To be able to look at your situation as fact and accept it, and still come up with things shows a remarkable strength of character. And Eki and many of the shibes have that strong character. Get out there and find something to do with Dogecoin.

Learn more about ShibeNet:
ShibeNet.org and reddit.com/r/shibenet

Support the v8 SuperDogeCar Project:
http://www.dogeraiser.com/c/25
DTHtAYbFZMBSmwzYnbHebBLVX5BNQUSkjj

Follow the project on Twitter with the hashtag:
#Dogev8

LUNAR IDITAROD

DREAM

AMAZE, SO LISTEN

TOM BOICE

Autoration in concert

As the music columnist for VERYMUCHWOW, it behooves me to explore the great musicians we have right here in the Dogecoin community.

One of my favorite artists that I discovered through the ĐTunes Store (https://sites.google.com/site/dogetunes/) is **Autorotation**, a melodic-electronic trio from London. Autorotation has a gift for blending acoustic emotion and catchy-but-glitchy electronica, providing a stimulating and enjoyable listening experience.

Originally formed in 2001, Autorotation finds their inspiration in ambient sounds and society - two ideals that fall in line with Dogecoin's emphasis on community and inclusion. Through our interaction, I learned that they are drawn to Dogecoin for its vibrant community that built a functional digital economy, while not taking itself too seriously.

My personal favorite song by the trio is "*Autorrhea*," for it's lyrics and acoustics that walk a thin line between tension and relaxation, like trying to sleep the night before your own wedding. "*Icen Glow*" is equally great, having a poppy energy and mesmerizing layered melodies. Also, I'm a sucker

for the horns near the end of the song. I had the pleasure of getting to ask them about their music, and what drew the group to Dogecoin.

Overall, it was a great time getting to speak with Autorotation, and I would encourage you purchase their music (with Dogecoin), and definitely keep an eye on their new project **The Split**, www.thesplit.info. Here is the full text of our exchange:

TB: *So, how did Dogecoin first enter your radar, and why did you decide to being selling your music for Dogecoin? (as opposed to other digital currencies like Bitcoin)*

Igor: Being a long-time Reddit lurker, I was aware of the Doge meme for a while. Then a friend told me that he was dealing with Bitcoin as an investment opportunity, so I decided to have a look. Well, Bitcoin and other similar currencies looked like potentially good investments, but did not appear to be live and vibrant currencies that people use to buy and sell, like you would with a traditional currency.

That was the appeal of Dogecoin: the Dogecoin subreddit is always so positive, friendly and not very serious. People seem to want it to become a real alternative to traditional currency. All of which aligns well with our political views as a band, so we decided to try Dogecoin

TB: *What inspires Autorotation to make music?*

Igor: Lyrically, we talk about one of the most important relationships of all: society, and the politics that govern it. Well, we do sing about other things as well, but politics and economics are at the forefront, so you could say that watching news inspires the lyrics.

Musically, we are simply inspired by the sounds (musical and otherwise) that we hear around us – from the construction noises outside to the latest glitch EP by a net label.

TB: *You have talked about how the group is interested in music-making software and integrating it into performance, is there a specific method you use for designing a performance? Do you have a specific goal in mind when you're looking for software to use in live performance?*

Igor: Each performance has it's own software setup which needs to be prepared. We select the key interactive elements and then program the interfaces to allow us to control the software in an intuitive way. The goal is to make this interaction as immediate and spontaneous as possible.

TB: *Does each of you have a favorite song to perform? Which one/s? Why?*

Laura: I must say I'm enjoying "*Ginger Pants*," which alternates between delicate glockenspiel and the rolling rhythms of the floor tom. Its like a traveling caravan of strange and beautiful creatures

Igor: "*Autorrhea*," because I get to play the guitar and samba drums in the same song.

Robyn: I guess I enjoy "*Mittelschmerz*" because of the way the multiple vocal lines intertwine.

TB: Do you have any thoughts on the future of Dogecoin, or digital currency in general?

Igor: I'm hoping that Dogecoin in particular will become a real, live and dynamic alternative that will drive an independent online economy, as opposed to being an abstract commodity of speculative investment.

TB: *What is in the works for Autorotation? Any upcoming releases we can be excited about?*

Igor: We are organizing a mini-festival this summer in a chapel in South-East London. Also, our international pop/rock side project, **The Split**, has just been released. We are also busy writing new material for the new release.

AUTOROTATION

VISIT US AT AUTOROTATION.ORG

Tip Tom:

D76r9vZeJTE6FGmharckyo1ZiYn4bdxTmJ

ROBERTMCGRATH

VERYMUCHWOW INTERVIEWS COMPUTER SCIENTIST ROBERT MCGRATH

Robert E. McGrath is a retired software engineer and social scientist, currently interested in digitally augmented communities and IT that strengthens local communities. He blogs and writes about various topics, including augmented reality, personal fabrication, "the future of work", and cryptocurrency communities. He lives in Urbana, Illinois.

Blog: http://robertmcgrath.wordpress.com/

Tell us about your interest in cryptocurrency.

I am retired. I was a computer programmer for many years. Even before the internet, I was involved in discussions about virtual currencies; it's always been something I've had an interest in.

My first degree was in Anthropology. I tend to be interested in how people are using the computer, and how people are interested in the ways they connect within that space.

The Bitcoin community is rough and ready, and I'm not attracted by the community's Libertarian tendencies. I ran across Dogecoin. It's the same technology by a totally different vibe. The underlying technology is one thing, and the community behind it is another. My anthropology antennae lit off and thought this was interesting.

What kinds of things interest you in the various communities?

There is a new cryptocurrency every day, it seems. Sometimes more than one. I've identified a bunch of interesting cases, and I'm examining how these things are technologically the same but have a different idea behind them. New ones are born, and some "older" ones are dying.

Look at MazaCoin, for example. It is designed to be the national currency of the Lakota nation. The man who designed it says he wants to have it imbibed with cultural pride, economic development, etc. There are a number of coins in this new social activism space. This is a very old cultural narrative being set up with the cultural narrative of the day.

What kinds of topics do you cover in your blog?

I write about how the differences in the technology are nil. There are small differences in the exact math problems used for mining, the parameters etc - but these are very tiny compared to other things. Whatever is going on in terms of community is not driven by the technology. Some people are jumping back and forth.

The other implication is that the world doesn't need these things. It's so easy to make a coin. Where's the first feminist coin? As an anthropologist and a computer scientist, these are interesting questions.

I'm trying to put my observations and things I've learned into perspective. Mining is a horrible ecological waste, one of the worst things about the entire enterprise. Why is it necessary? There are other ways one could create coins that wouldn't steal from our energy resources.

Do you invest in any cryptocurrencies?

I've only handled a few hundred coins at

a time, mostly to play with the softare and see how and if it works. I've been much more interested in what people are saying, and the plays that they are acting out using the currencies.

I would guess that "grownups" will get ahold of it, and big bands will make a form of it that they run, a form that the government supervises. At that point, it will replace credit cards.

Why is Dogecoin so interesting to you?

From the start, the Dogecoin community was about totally different things. First, they were not so serious. They ignore speculation and focus on tipping and charity. They like sharing funny things. There is this massive industry of dog pictures coming out of the community. There is no justification for that except that there is a community doing this, and it is a unifying theme that brings people together.

DOING RIGHT BY DOUGLAS ADAMS: BUILDING THE REAL WORLD INFINITE IMPROBABILITY ENGINE OR "THE DOGECOIN DRIVE"

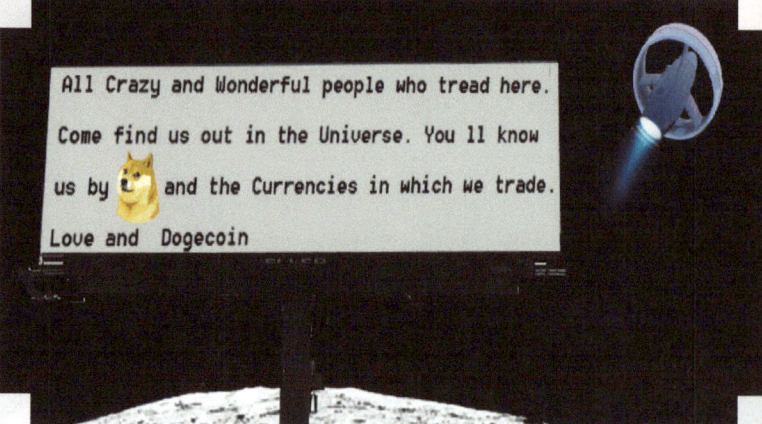

All Crazy and Wonderful people who tread here. Come find us out in the Universe. You'll know us by [doge] and the Currencies in which we trade. Love and Dogecoin

The infinite improbability drive is a wonderful new method of crossing interstellar distances in a mere nothingth of a second, without all that tedious mucking about in hyperspace. It was discovered by lucky chance, and then developed into a governable form of propulsion by the Galactic Government's research center on Damogran.

Hitchhiker Wiki, topic: Infinite Improbability Drive

I maintain this is not a science fiction, but a science fact as made real by Dogecoin, the digital currency.

Turn on the Improbability Drive for a second... against all probability a sperm whale had suddenly been called into existence several miles above the surface of an alien planet. And since this is not a naturally tenable position for a whale, this poor innocent creature had very little time to come to terms with its identity as a whale before it then had to come to terms with not being a whale any more. This is a complete record of its thoughts from the moment it began its life till the moment it ended it, "Ah ... ! What's happening? it thought. Er, excuse me, who am I? Hello? Why am I here? What's my purpose in life? What do I mean by who am I? What's this thing? This ... let's call it a tail - yeah, tail. Hey! I can can really thrash it about pretty good can't I? Wow! Wow! That feels great! Doesn't seem to achieve very much but I'll probably find out what it's for later on... And wow! Hey! What's this thing suddenly coming towards me very fast? Very very fast. So big and flat and round, it needs a big wide sounding name like ... ow ... ound ... round ... ground! That's it! That's a good name - ground! I wonder if it will be friends with me?" And the rest, after a sudden wet thud, was silence. Curiously enough, the only thing that went through the mind of the bowl of petunias as it fell was, "Oh no, not again."

Improbable things happen in the universe, not with great frequency but with regularity in proportion to their likeliness. This is a concept that people should understand but have trouble with intuitively, in practice. That is to say, people think because a thing is one in a million that "it never happens." Uh-uh, that ain't right. It happens exactly one in a million times on average. If you are looking for a one in a million thing to happen and you give it a million chances and don't see it take place, something has gone as wrong as clown sex featuring balloons. In fact, when we don't see something unlikely after a great number of chances have passed, that should be the unlikely thing, and a clue to us that something is wrong in our original premise.

Another thing they couldn't stand was the perpetual failure they encountered in trying to construct a machine which could generate the infinite improbability field needed to flip a spaceship across the mind-paralysing distances between the furthest stars, and in the end they grumpily announced that such a machine was virtually impossible.

Then, one day, a student who had been left to sweep up the lab after a particularly unsuccessful party found himself reasoning this way: If, he thought to himself, such a machine is a virtual impossibility, then it must logically be a finite improbability. So all I have to do in order to make one is to work out exactly how improbable it is, feed that figure into the finite improbability generator, give it a fresh cup of really hot tea ... and turn it on! He did this, and was rather startled to discover that he had managed to create the long sought after golden Infinite Improbability generator out of thin air. (Adams 32)

With fact established let's look back at dogecoin and see how it's applicable. Now people are trained such that "unlikely things just don't happen" as I said because in life they rarely happen and that gives life a plenty of time, plenty of chance to poison our pattern recognizing mind with the idea that it's never going to happen, on average. So we have a whole culture of "exciting things never happen to me" and "I'm never the lucky one." Which is just flat wrong. People who think this way aren't looking for, aren't putting themselves in the position to, take advantage of opportunity when it comes their way. Which is just as bad as saying "no" to it and slamming the door in its face. This is the crucial thing that shibes understand that many other people do not. The odds against aren't infinite, just substantial. So with a lot of work and a little luck--not an unreasonable amount, mind you--you can cajole the unlikely into happening. And so with dogecoin we have a culture dedicated to turning this idea on it's head, centered around obtaining the unlikely and putting it to work for them. I think this is just as splendid as giant sexy holographic robots riding battleships through a series of bacon and cheese flavored explosions.

It says: Sensational new breakthrough in Improbability Physics. As soon as the ship's drive reaches Infinite Improbability it passes through every point in the Universe. Be the envy of other major governments. Wow, this is big league stuff. (Adams 35)

And so we can go to the moon, for real. We are actually doing so, I suppose you've read by now. And we will be there in person eventually. And I posit that we will go a lot farther: anywhere our beautiful, ridiculous minds will take us (Birdie said, "Mars, Europa" upon hearing the moon news, but even that is not grand enough--to Alpha Centauri and beyond right up to the edge of the observable universe, and that's where our real work will begin!). Yes, we have to stop saying "to the moon!" now I think; it's limiting. "Past the moon? Beyond the moon?", you will come up with the right thing, I've no doubt.

This was when the first major muddles of Galactic history set in, with battles continually re-erupting centuries after the issues they had been fought over had supposedly been settled. However, these muddles were as nothing to the ones which historians had to try and unravel once time-travel was discovered and battles started pre-erupting hundreds of years before the issues even arose. When the Infinite Improbability Drive arrived and whole planets started turning unexpectedly into banana fruitcake, the great history faculty of the University of MaxiMegalon finally gave up, closed itself down and surrendered its buildings to the rapidly growing joint faculty of Divinity and Water Polo, which had been after them for years. (Adams 483)

And we are doing so in the best way too with principles of universal love and inclusion and empathy. This is really something... People are skeptical we will ever have the utopia envisioned in Star Trek, but I have no doubts. Dogecoin is going to save the world. The rocket is shaking right now (just as an aside), but all rockets do upon lift-off. Things will stabilize, and we'll be living "salad days" from here on out. Mom was right when she told us "love can do anything!" through her divorced ass teeth patronizingly to our little selves. Call her and tell her that you love her, you terrible ingrate!

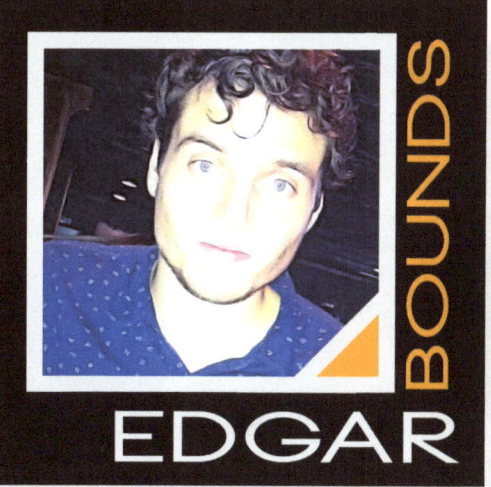

EDGAR BOUNDS

Tip Edgar:
DNH3qpWvonHXpFenecb56oHjb999wBzHYC

Cathy Keth's Doge4Education Bahay Kubo huts in progress.

7QUESTIONS

7QUESTIONS FOR CATHYKETH

Cathy Keth - /u/cathyketh on reddit - is an incredible member of ShibeNet. She is rescuing street children in her native Philippines and giving them opportunities to get an education. She answer VMW's questions about her charity fund, Doge4Education.

Tell us about Doge4Education.

If we can reach our target goal, three homeless children will get the opportunity to go to a nice school here in the Philippines for 8 years. They will receive a full scholarship with all expense paid. 100%! That could change their lives forever. That's the important thing.

These children feel that they are worthless. I want to help them make their lives better, and to feel that they are a vital part of our community. They need to know that they are loved, respected, and can keep learning. That is why I've created this charity work for them

Education is important all over the whole world. For me, personally, I have learned a lot in school and met many friends. I enjoyed my time in school, and I want these kids to have the same opportunities that I was able to have.

I know that if our Dogecoin community pulls together, we can make this dream come true for these children. The amount we need to raise is so small compared to the Dogecars, Doge4Water, and other funds. We can do this!

This is such a great project. What can the community do to help?

It would be great if we could get some community attention on the project. I can't control the Dogecoin community. I can only keep talking about the project and keep bringing it up for others to learn about.

How much do you need to raise to make this happen for these children?

We need $2200.00 to make this happen. We have raised $419.00 so far.

How did you first learn about Dogecoin?

I saw it on Facebook and then googled it. I started participating in the community and posting comments in the inspirational threads every day. I started giving away dogecoins because people tipped them to me. I am so happy when I am participating in the community. I love it.

Tell us about the children you hope to help. What are their lives like?

They are street children. But now some of them have someplace to sleep thanks to Josh Mohland and the community. We raised funds for the Bahay Kubo project which allowed us to build huts for them. The children we still need to reach sleep on the street. They don't have food.

How many more children need help?

For now we are focusing on three kids. After we get them the help they need, we can focus on more.

Have you lived in the Philippines all of your life?

Yes! I was born here.

Do you see a future for Dogecoin in the Philippines?

Of course! I can see Dogecoin logo everywhere in the future here in the Philippines. Dogecoin can change the lives of many people, and can uplift more lives.

Dogecoin can make our community a better place here in the Philippines.

To Learn More and to Donate: http://dogetipbot.wordpress.com/2014/04/30/dogetipbot-charity-updates/

On the DOGECONOMY

What is an idea worth?

On its own, nothing. To anyone who's been around long enough to know, ideas are nothing special on their own. They're seeds, yes, but they need fertile ground in which to grow.

Carefully cultivated - tended, protected, nurtured - an idea can change the world.

And Dogecoin stands ready to do exactly that... if we can make the leap across one, treacherous but necessary chasm.

A functioning DOGEconomy - well, any kind of functioning Economy, really - is one of the hardest things to build and yet it is one of the most important for our continued growth as a currency. The ability to use our coins and for them to be sent along the chain to be re-used instead of sold on the markets for USD or Euros or GBP is one of the great undertakings of our era. Finding businesses that will accept Dogecoin is one issue, but finding businesses that will hold it, instead of cashing it out; finding businesses that

are willing to restock other businesses in exchange for their DOGEs instead of Fiat currencies, that is a whole other ballpark entirely.

But the benefits of growing our DOGEconomy are legion and worth the effort - by creating a circular flow of Dogecoin within our businesses, we 'tie up' a portion of the Dogecoins that are mined within the system, creating a stable base demand which helps ensure that our valuation, the buying power of our coin, isn't merely tied to speculation. Furthermore, if those of us who are mining DOGE keep our Dogecoin flowing to businesses and to tipping others instead of letting them sit on exchanges, then we really start to see the simple principles of supply and demand come into play.

There are many ways to help bring about these changes, but most of the ones, specifically the ones that have the greatest chance of having a long-term positive effect are what one might call 'small' starts. Reaching out locally. I

know there are efforts to try and bring big names like Valve and such into the fold, to have them natively accept Dogecoin as payment -- and those are all wonderful efforts -- but sometimes thinking smaller, working locally really is the best possible option.

Some of our biggest successes thus far have been with small eateries with a strong foothold in the local community. The Iron Rail Diner (http://www.ironraildiner.com/), based out of Mount Savage, Maryland, has earned a significant bump in press coverage and support from the community for going all-in on Dogecoin.

Their 'Dips for Doge' summer Ice Cream program for kids raised over 300,000 Dogecoins from the community - enough to provide 225 ice cream cones for local kids. If that doesn't help to build a positive association with our coin, I don't know what will.

Another great success for Dogecoin takes us over to London, England with Burger

Bear. Tom, the owner of the Burger Bear food stand has earned himself a reputation for great food and good fun with the locals in Shoreditch. He'd started accepting all major forms of Cryptocurrency early on to try and help him increase awareness for his business, but it ended up being the Dogecoin crowd that really took the ball and ran with it, so to speak.

The community began by buying burgers for the homeless over Twitter and with Dogecoin, and that itself caused a Twitter storm which ended up with well over 300,000 Dogecoins being donated to help feed the locals. On Tom's birthday, no less.

It's little moments like this, moments where we make business owners and the communities they serve happy to accept our coin, excited to be able to tap into our Dogecoin community, that truly help

to cement the validity of our currency into the hearts and minds of people who might not have ever heard of us. And the bonus part? Both of these companies have decided to hold their Dogecoins instead of selling them for cash on the markets.

So, how can you get started? Perhaps the best way is to find local startups and small but successful eateries and, instead of asking them to accept Dogecoin for all purchases, ask them to consider a 'Dogecoin special.' Sell one item, or a special kind of item, for Dogecoin only. See if it gets them any attention, if there's any demand. If there's no demand, it hasn't cost them anything. It's through setting up small footholds like this, though creating connections with small communities and making positive impacts there, all over the world, that our currency can start to truly build a foothold out

in the real world as well.

By giving those who use our currency more choices and more outlets to spend their coins - and actively supporting those businesses that welcome them - we can start to realize our dream of building a functional, cyclical, Dogecoin economy.

It's going to take some ingenuity and a good bit of hard work, but luckily that's pretty much what we're known for.

Tip GoodShibe:
DH6hKwqsKuDDy3S9jES5VDJfLdyJgY1j7E

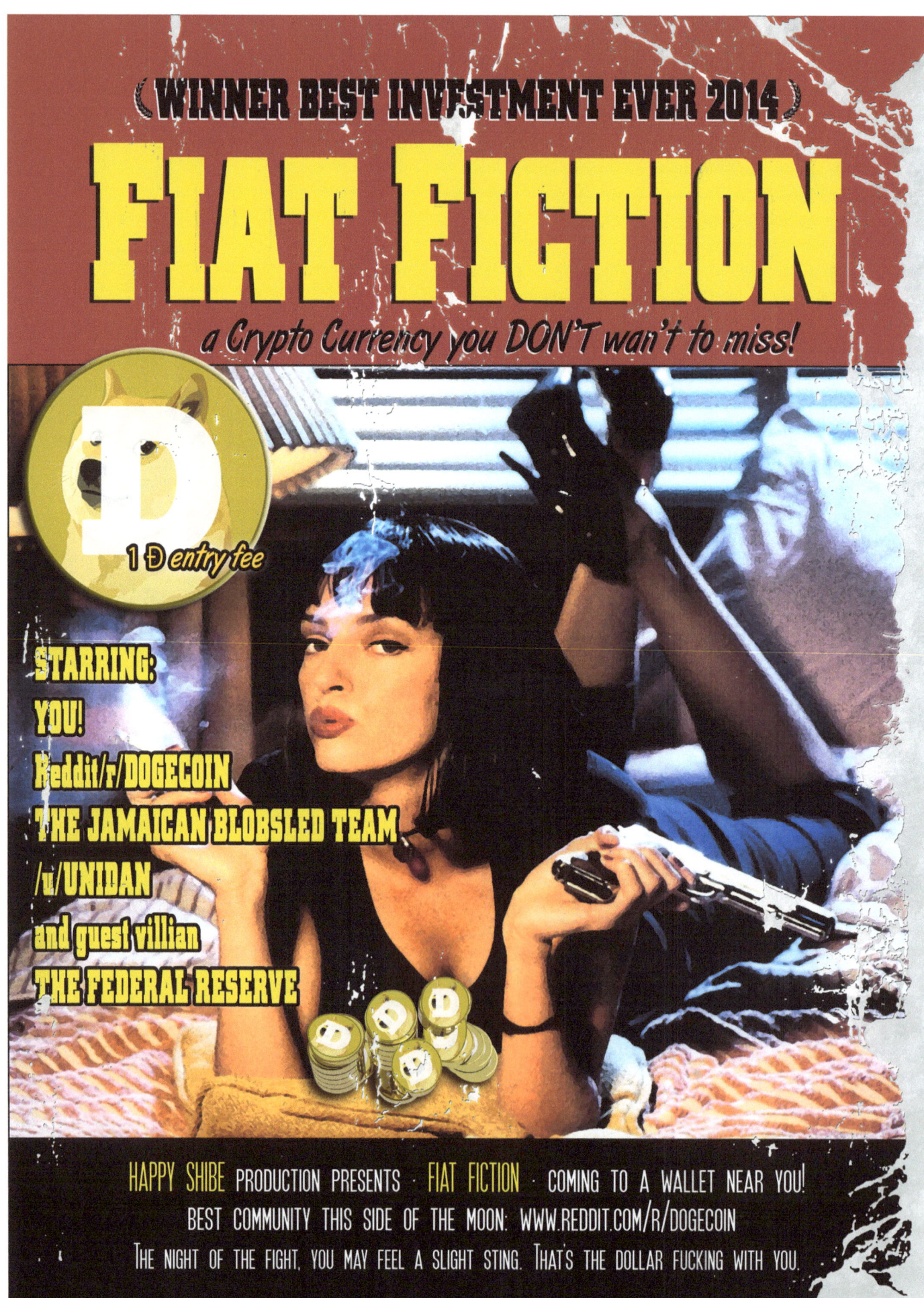

IF YOU BARK ON THE MOON, DOES A SHIBE HEAR?

MOON PARTY

STARRING

JEAN-LUC PICARD · LUKE SKYWALKER · ET · DREW BARRYMORE · CHER

DOGE AFTER DARK

email DogeAfterDark@VeryMuchWow.com with your
midnight rantings and moonlit thoughts...

Middle of the night crazy ideas... Are your legs twitching while you dream? Do you feel like howling at the moon? Send us your Doge After Dark Dreams, Rants, and Moonlit Ideas. For our June issue, a well-known and bombastic www.reddit.com/r/dogecoin member sent in a "Stray Doge" rant... Don't agree? Send in your own!

I am getting tired of the Dogecoin subreddit. Every time I post something cool, it effectively vanishes after 10 minutes. The sub moves too damned fast. And now we have these downvote bots who just love to kill a thread in three seconds flat. What's the point of these bots, anyway?

Another reason I'm tired of /r/dogecoin: too many fatuous, pompous, preachy shibes who thinks that platitudes make the man. You know what, mates? They just make you look like ineffectual jerks. You aren't going to make it past escape velocity if you insist on talking down to the rest of us. You know who you are.

Reason 3: all of these so-called "elections." WTF?! This is a decentralized currency, sweethheart. No one gives a flying you-know-what about your glorious goals. We are getting things done just fine without your "leadership."

Reason 4: The hand-slapping nature of some members. What's wrong with a little fun? This is reddit. This ain't Sunday School. Reddit isn't supposed to be "family friendly."

I don't want to lose the fun in the community which is why I am sending in this rant which you will probably delete.

Dear Mr. Doge,

I want to run for Dogecoin Emperor. What should I do?

Signed,
Call Me Your Highness

Dear "High,"

Dogecoin needs an Emperor like a fish needs a Milk Bone. Why not join the /r/pyongyang sub and fulfill your most wondrous Glorious Leader fantasies? Bonus: Introduce them to Dogecoin! Even North Korean apologists need a tip now and then!

Dear Mr. Doge,

I'm frustrated by the lack of shibettes in the community. What's a lonely shibe gotta do to get a date? I keep trying to invite the women I meet to try out Dogecoin, but I keep stumbling when I try to explain the "Blockchain." They think I'm into something I'm not. What do I do?

Signed,
Not Into The Leash

Dear Not-So-UnLeashed,

Where are you getting your demographics? We are a varied community with pure breds to mutts.

DOGE
ASK A

"I'm just a hot-blooded American Shibe. Got trouble? I give YOU the tips!"

email askadoge @verymuchwow.com with your sadness...

MUCH HELP

SUCH AMAZE ADVICE

<- Tip
Ask A Doge

Stop sniffing your own butt and get out thee and explore the outer reaches of the dog park! When you see a Shibette, don't try to act dominant. They can see through that behavior and you will be on their "list." You don't want to get on the list, man. Try tipping a shibette-friendly number of Doge - you know what numbers to avoid!

Dear Ask A Doge,

I appreciated that you answer a question from a cat last issue. It's good to see some extra-species activity in the community. Which brings me to my question: Are you a single doge or taken? Inquiring minds need to know.

Signed,
Could be cat. Could be mouse.

Dear Itchin' to Know,

One. I am a single and hot-blooded American shibe. Two. I like piña coladas, getting lost in the rain, homemade meat jerky, lasagna, belly rubs, chicken skin, name-brand kibbles, dirty socks, dumpster diving, a good howl now and then, licking other species' toes, and a classic rock album.
Three. How about this Saturday, 9 pm, behind Sal's Pizza Emporium?

AN INTERVIEW WITH ONLINE SHIBE RADIO STATION DOGEXM

VERY MUCH WOW spoke with Ben Butzow and Jeffrey Matthews II of DogeXM, an online 24-hour-a-day Dogecoin radio station. All artists on the channel accept Dogecoin donations for their work, and some accept payment in Dogecoin for their albums. If you love music and want to support artists who care about Dogecoin, tune in and enjoy an eclectic mix of shibe-created tunes, from classical to jazz to original electronic pieces.

VMW: How did you come up with DogeXM?

Ben: It started as an idea like, "Hey, there's all this stuff going on, why not make an online radio thing?"

Jeffrey: Ben was talking about having a radio show, and I was familiar with the artists on *Dogetunes.net*. We thought it would be a cool idea to start an online radio that played the music of those in the Dogecoin community.

VMW: What kind of music can you hear at DogeXM?

Jeffrey: We play acoustic and electronic music. At this point we have artists of all genres. You can visit the artists' Bandcamp, Soundcloud and Dogetunes sites to learn more about them. Listeners who like the music can buy it with dogecoins on Dogetunes.

How many listeners tune in to DogeXM?

Ben: The streaming service we use tells us that we have, on average, five at any given time.

How did you find musicians to feature?

Jeffrey: All the musicians are part of a group; we all talk to each other. We asked the community if anybody would like to have their music played at DogeXM. Within the first 24 hours, we had 17 different people. If someone is interested in having their music featured, we have a form at the site that they can fill out.

Ben: We have a thing called DogeXM live. We've done two things on it so far: a mix of electronic music, the **Shibe Showcase**, from each of the shibe artists at the time. Anyone can do a live mix, or if you have a podcast, you could have it air on DogeXM for the first time.

Do any artists use the Doge meme in their work?

Ben: I heard about all of our artists through Dogetunes. I've looked at some of their artwork. None of them are a Doge-specific artist. Some of them have references in their music - Stereo Odyssey has a song called "To the Moon," for example. Some others reference Dogecoin.

Who are your favorite artists on DogeXM?

Jeffrey: It's hard to pick favorites - everyone on DogeXM are all very talented artists. I like Stereo Odyssey. He does a lot of electronic music.

Ben: We're always looking for more artists to feature, more people to do things live on DogeXM.

Listen to Dogecoin artists at DogeXM.com

DO YOU HAVE A BUSINESS OR WEBSITE THAT FEATURES SHIBES? LET US KNOW!
EMAIL: EDITOR@VERYMUCHWOW.COM

BETWEEN THE
MOONS

GO DOGE!

For more info:
Dogecoin.com
Howtodoge.com

Communities:
Reddit.com/r/dogecoin
discuss.dogecoin.com

Birdie Jaworski ©2014

Dogecoin is a new digital currency,
that you may easily send across the Internet.
Quickly transfer cash from Amsterdam to
Albuquerque to Adelaide!

DOGECOIN IS EASY TO USE AND UNDERSTAND

Dogecoin is the perfect way to send money to people in your neighborhood - or across the world! You can send $0.10 to your favorite comment on Twitter, $10 to your favorite band for their latest album, or $100 to support your favorite charity.

Have a business? Are you an artist? You can directly accept digital cash rather than a simple "like." With Dogecoin, there's no middleman!

Be a part of the Dogecoin revolution!

Join the worldwide Dogecoin revolution!

Within months, Dogecoin has already funded Olympic athletes, clean water in Africa, and a NASCAR sponsorship.

Our community is welcoming and generous! You'll fit right in.

TO JOIN IN:

1 Download a wallet from Dogecoin.com for your phone, computer, or tablet. A Dogecoin Wallet is software that holds dogecoins.

2 Install & Sync with the Dogecoin network

3 Wallet addresses look like "DXXX" and are used to receive dogecoins. Find your address in your wallet under "Receive." To receive payments, just let people know your wallet address.

4 When you have received some dogecoins, spend them by sending to a destination address!

You might see Dogecoin addresses in QR code form - scan them!

JUNE CRAFT PROJECT: DOGECOIN COOTIE CATCHER!

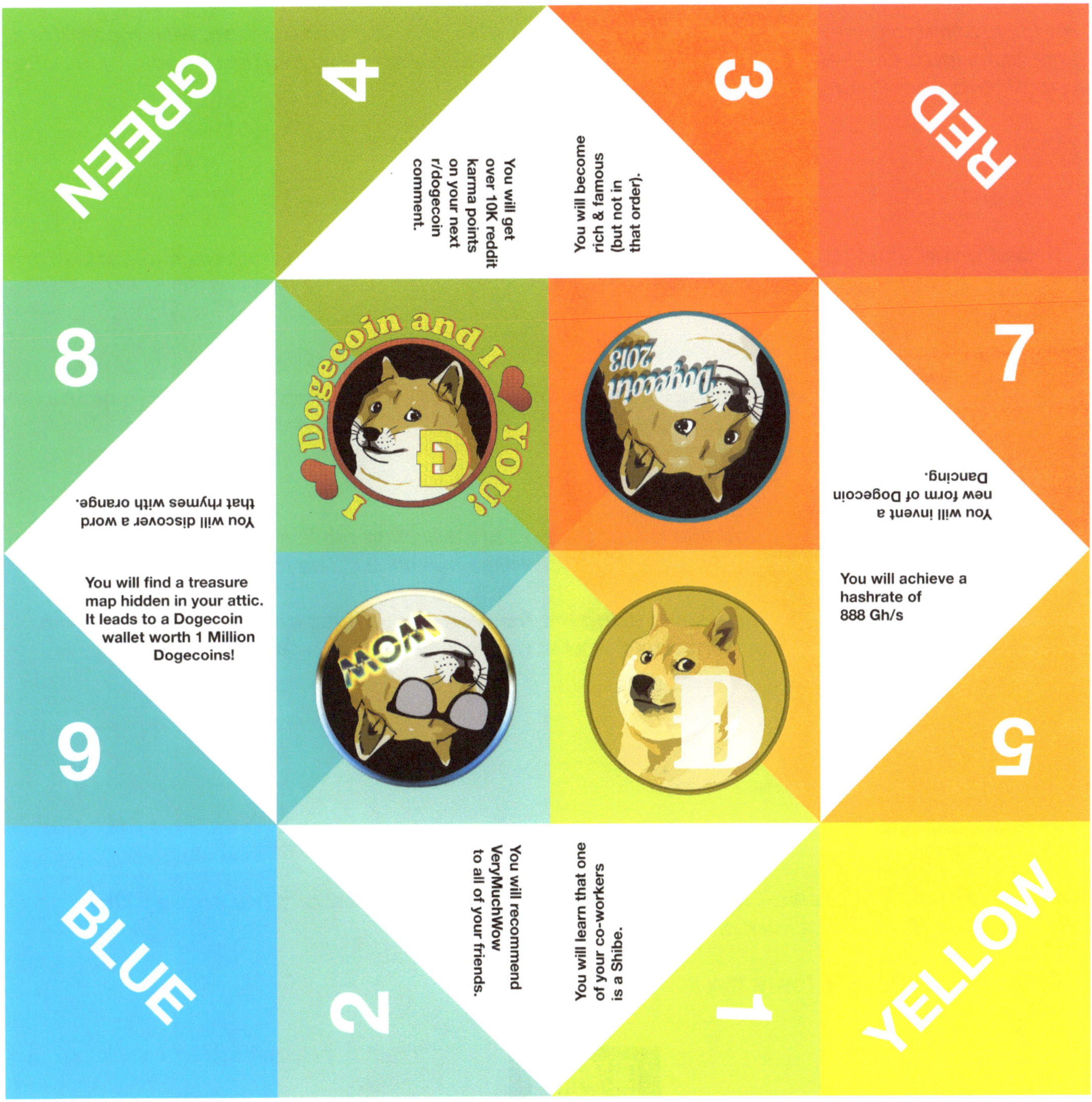

GREEN

4

You will get over 10K reddit karma points on your next r/dogecoin comment.

3

You will become rich & famous (but not in that order).

RED

8

You will discover a word that rhymes with orange.

You will find a treasure map hidden in your attic. It leads to a Dogecoin wallet worth 1 Million Dogecoins!

7

You will invent a new form of Dogecoin Dancing.

You will achieve a hashrate of 888 Gh/s

9

BLUE

2

You will recommend VeryMuchWow to all of your friends.

You will learn that one of your co-workers is a Shibe.

1

YELLOW

5

Love crafts? Send in a craft story, photo, idea, or template and get published in VeryMuchWow!
You will be paid 20K Doge for your selected submission!
Send an inquiry to: editor@verymuchwow.com

The Last Man on Earth

many words

The last man on Earth sat alone in a room. There was a knock on the door.

I sat up in fear, my body tense, ready.

Damn it.

I had the same dream every night for three weeks straight, the same dream with me stuffed in my grandpa's La-Z-Boy, the same dream with that same strange muffled knock. I just didn't expect to dream it again. Not here.

I winced.

"Lights on."

I climbed down from the slumber bay and padded across the control pod. No messages from Houston.

"Lights off."

The computer complied, and I stared through the wrap-around screen, into space, stared at the slowly vanishing blue ball. It was only hours since lift-off, but it felt like months.

FLASH!

Ice white light cascaded around the back of my craft, blinding me for a few seconds. I grabbed the console as the shock wave hit, steadied myself for the inevitable tumble.

The asteroid flew into the space separating me from my home. Just another day in fricken space, I thought. I climbed back into bed and strapped myself in for the long flight, let my eyelids drop.

KNOCK!

I sat up in fear, my body tense, ready.

Damn it.

Wait. This wasn't the dream. I leaned deep to one side and looked out the screen. Tiny particles flew from the center of a missing planet.

I sat, alone in the room. I was the last man from Earth.

Original Flash Fiction by Josepha K.

Tip Josepha:
DD8cSCpP7P7Y6iJpjuhmKZjhLLGF4zytJq

The Dog and the Ghost Sickness

My mother handed me a dress, a handmade swirl of red and green woven cloth with a full skirt. Stars seemed to hang a little lower, seemed to hover between the earth and sky. I could almost touch them when I raised my arms. My oily dark hair was fashioned into a special knot and fastened with the carved bone of a deer's thigh.

I remember the shift of desert sand beneath my feet as the shaman began the first of the twelve hogan songs of the Bahózhonchi. His voice echoed in the same plane as the stars, shot toward the unruly dots of light the anglos call planets. My soul became tied with plant, with stone, with the string of ancient ancestors hunting through the milky belt across the sky. I could hear the raspy breath of my great-great auntie, could smell her breath, the acrid stench of the confusing stop between life and death.

It was when the medicine man began the second song that The Dog arrived. He ran into the circle, twirled three times, then ran straight to me. Dust rose into the glow from the fire, seemed to form the simple shapes of the kachinas. The chanting continued, but all of the women looked at the animal. It had to be a sign. He looked like every other dog on the reservation - gaunt, mangy, with a body full of heat and anger. He stood, nose to my chest, as if he were checking for my heartbeat.

"Jahona." My great-great auntie wheezed my name. I shivered in the near-freezing air. "Jahona."

The Dog kept his nose pressed against my new dress. No one made a move to shoo him from the circle. You don't reject a sign from the other world.

"Jahona. Listen to me." My auntie erupted in a coughing fit, but the medicine man continued his work. I knew I couldn't move, wasn't allowed to move, not yet.

"This dog is a gift from Father Sky. I saw a star fall and made a wish for you right before the dog ran into the power."

I called him Hok'ee. Abandoned. Hok'ee.

Hok'ee acted as though he knew me forever, knew me in my past life as a child, knew me in the future as an old woman. You have to understand - the relationship of a dog to a man, to a woman, is not the same with the Navajo as it is to the white man. Not those days. Dogs are in the natural world, and we must navigate the changing landscape between the world we can contain in our mind and the world that we manage with our hands.

Those days we kept dogs the way you keep ants in your home. They exist; they live in harmony, sometimes in disharmony. But they were not something to coddle or pet. They worked for their dinner, caught their own meat. It is the way of life. A dog has a deep hunger, a need to roam.

Hok'ee roamed like the other dogs on the reservation. He liked to steal chickens, like to grab eggs, catch rabbit and snake. At least once a day he would sit near me and I would watch the fleas rise and fall with his breath. Rough skin bristled under his coat, a crisscross of scar and wayward tufts of fur.

One day my mother told me to collect sage and cholla fruit, so I headed toward the mesa. Hok'ee met me halfway, ran ahead on the well-worn desert path. All animals know the way to the best harvest. I carried a sturdy basket woven from piñon needles. Under the sun it exuded a heavenly scent, and I breathed deeply, over and over, wanted to capture the smell forever in my lungs.

Blip!

I caught something in the corner of my eye, a flash, but it sparked too fast for me to see. I scanned the horizon for Hok'ee, but couldn't see him in any direction.

Blip!

The flash happened again, this time to my right, and when I turned, Hok'ee trotted next to me, eyes focused on the mesa.

In the desert, a minute lasts an hour. The sun can play tricks on your mind, can make you see and forget things. The blip had to be a combination of

cont'd on next page ->

too much pine scent, too many heavy breaths, not enough water. When we reached the mesa, I bit into a bitter cholla and sucked out the sweet juice. My belly shook in appreciation. An hour later, my basket stretched full with the tough yellow fruit, with several large handfuls of fragrant sage. I lifted it to my head and balanced it, my back straight and true, and began the trek home, the sun to our back.

Hok'ee had caught a quail while I foraged, and I could see bits of blood around his jaw as he led the way back to the hogan.

"Jahona!"

My older brother ran to meet me. He was almost a warrior. He kept Navy photographs under his sleeping mat. He hadn't told my father and mother that he wanted to join the service, to see the endless salty waters that none of us quite believed existed.

"Hand me your basket. Run! Run, girl! Run! The boy with the spot has joined the ancestors."

I froze in place, couldn't move, didn't understand. The little boy lived in a hogan close to ours. His left arm was covered in an enormous port wine stain, so he was known - as we all were - by our most distinct characteristic.

"How?"

I ran, tried to catch up to my brother. Miguel slowed his pace to match mine. The basket swung in the fading light. I hit a small branch of spiky goatheads with my feet and winced, stopped to pick the briars out of my soles. I lost sight of Hok'ee.

My question was foolish. The People don't like to discuss death. It is anathema to us, it is unholy. We fear death, fear the remnants of the transition. We bury our dead immediately; they carry evil.

"They think coyote. He had bite marks everywhere."

Hok'ee didn't return for many days. I didn't think much of it. The dogs come and go on the reservation. They sometimes wander in packs, like the coyote, sometimes hunt for mule deer and antelope. Every once in a while I thought I saw something out of the corner of my eye, thought I saw a blip, a flash, a hint of something the vision can't savor.

Another child in the village died, this time of measles. Welts spread across her belly until she looked like a gaunt reservation dog. Then a wasp stung one of my cousins, a teenaged girl, and she died, too. One of my uncles broke his legs when his horse spooked at something invisible. An old woman across the dry wash said

something knocked the back of her lower legs, and she fell into her root cellar, shattering her back, leaving her paralyzed.

It didn't take me long to see the pattern. Blip. Flash. Death. Blip. Flash. Pain. I remembered the journey to the mesa. I remembered Hok'ee, the viscous blood between his teeth.

A chindi. He was a chindi. A ghost left behind when someone dies. A ghost who carries others into the ghostlands.

The moment I held the thought I saw something rustle out of the corner of my eye. Blip. Flash. Hok'ee panted in the distance, the first time I'd seen him in months. A lone crow cawed above me, a warning.

Chindi don't die; they are already dead. Hok'ee sauntered closer. Blood dripped from his jaw, onto his paws. Miguel ran up behind me carrying a knapsack full of everything he owned. He hugged me tight, but in his excitement to ride in the back of a rancher's pickup to the city, to begin his basic training, he didn't notice the fear in my expression.

"You be good to nuestra madre, mi hermanita," he grinned. He slung the pack over one shoulder and ran down the dirt road. I watched him until I could see him no more.

Blip. Flash. Hok'ee disappeared.

Miguel never returned home. Hok'ee never did, either. He must have found fresher meat, must have figured that we were crippled enough, damaged enough to kill our own.

Sometimes people bring dogs into the nursing home. They think that the old and dying would like to pet something soft and gentle, but I know what lurks beneath the fur. The dog is a guardian of both worlds, but a slave to his belly. He will serve the master who offers the best catch. He walks beside us, a companion of opportunity. He waits.

FOR OUR JULY ISSUE:

SUBMIT ORIGINAL POETRY FEATURING DOGECOIN, SHIBES, SPACE, MOON, THE IDEA OF VALUE, ECONOMY, OR TRADE.

Send your original poetry to:

editor@verymuchwow.com

by Not-So-Anonymous
Please tip the artists and writers in this magazine - they deserve it! I don't! :)

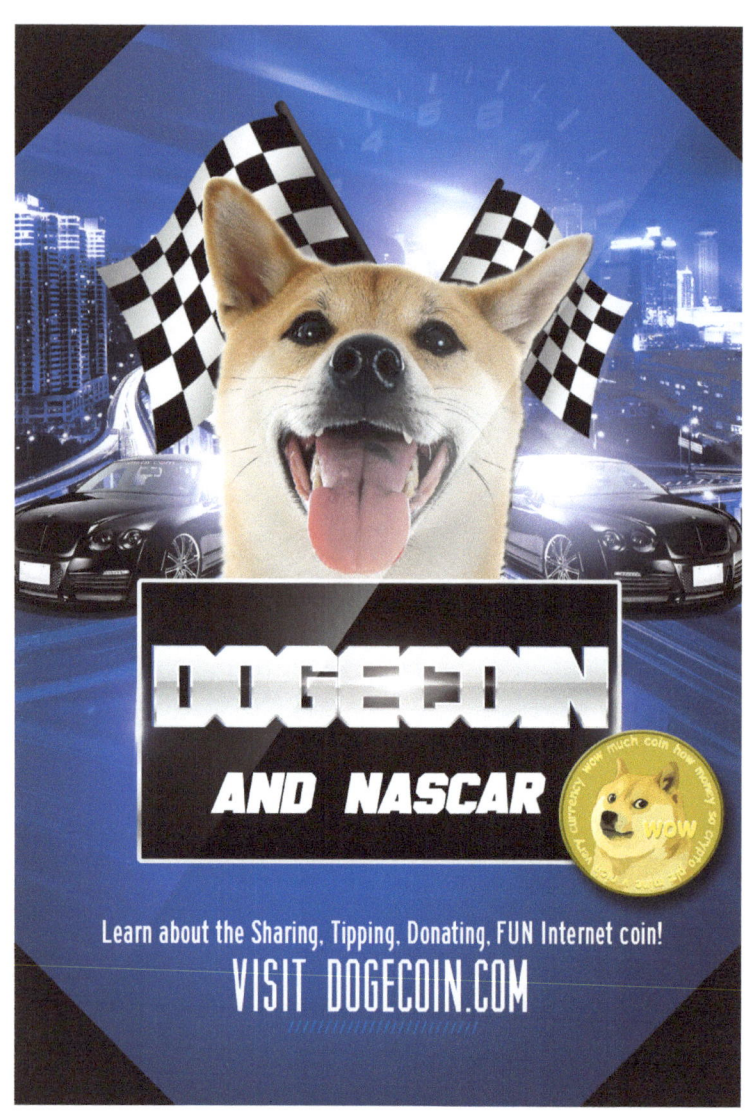

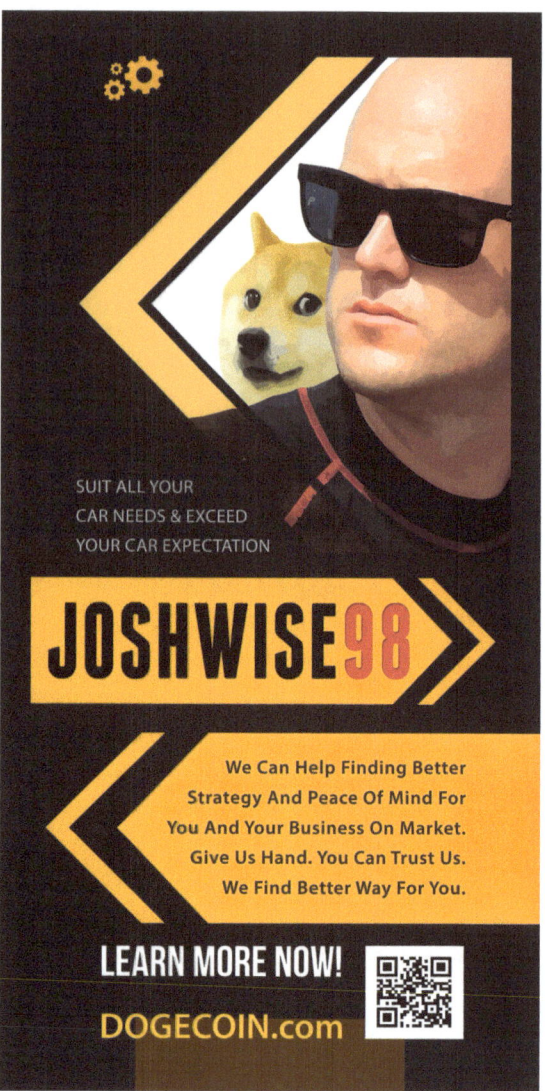

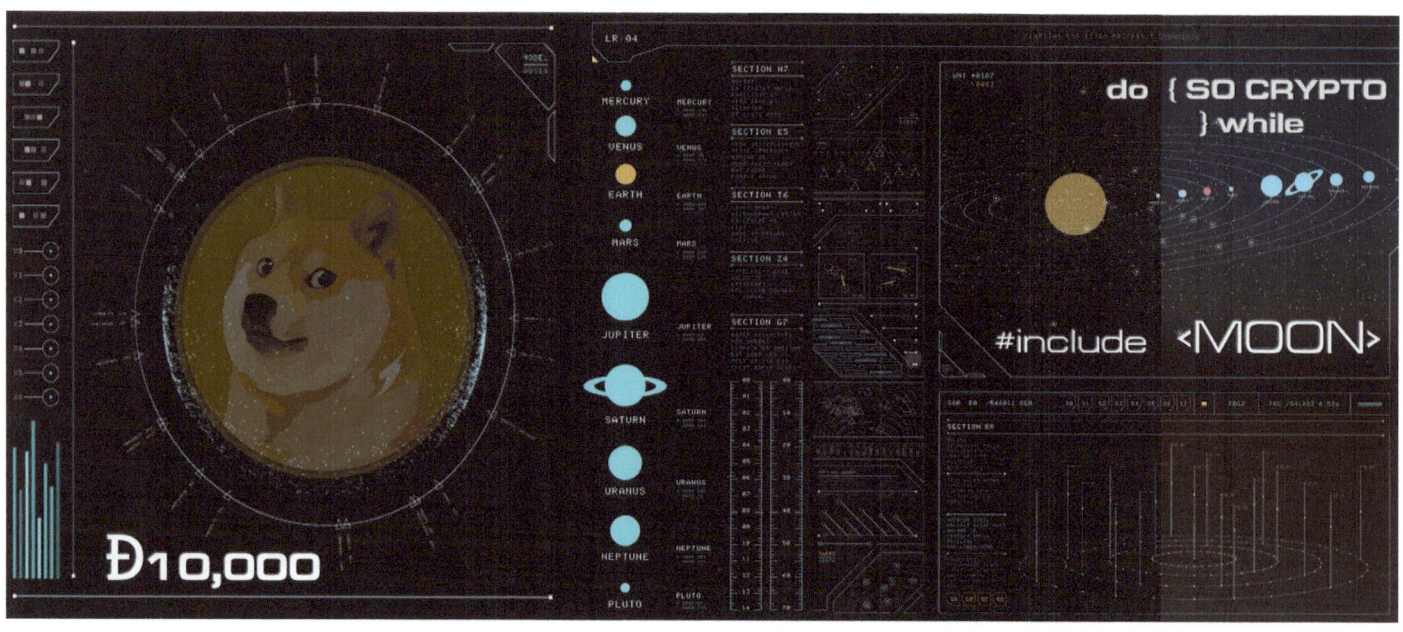

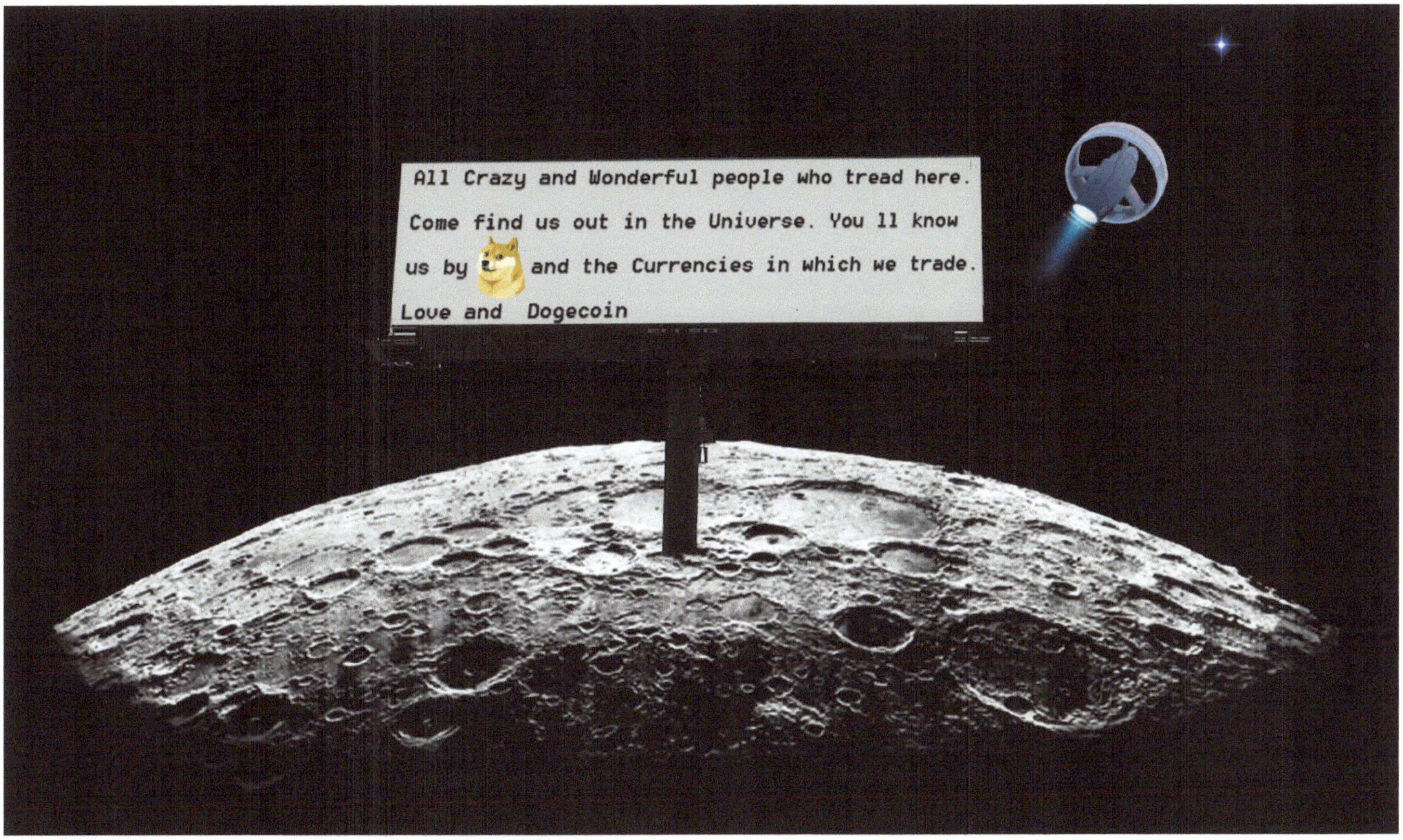

All Crazy and Wonderful people who tread here.
Come find us out in the Universe. You ll know
us by and the Currencies in which we trade.
Love and Dogecoin

Doge sign on the moon by Edgar Bounds

BECAUSE OF DOGECOIN
THE
MOON
For ALL Of Us
verymuchwow.com

IN DOGE
WE TRUST
WoooooooooooooF
SUCH COIN
TOSS ME A BONE

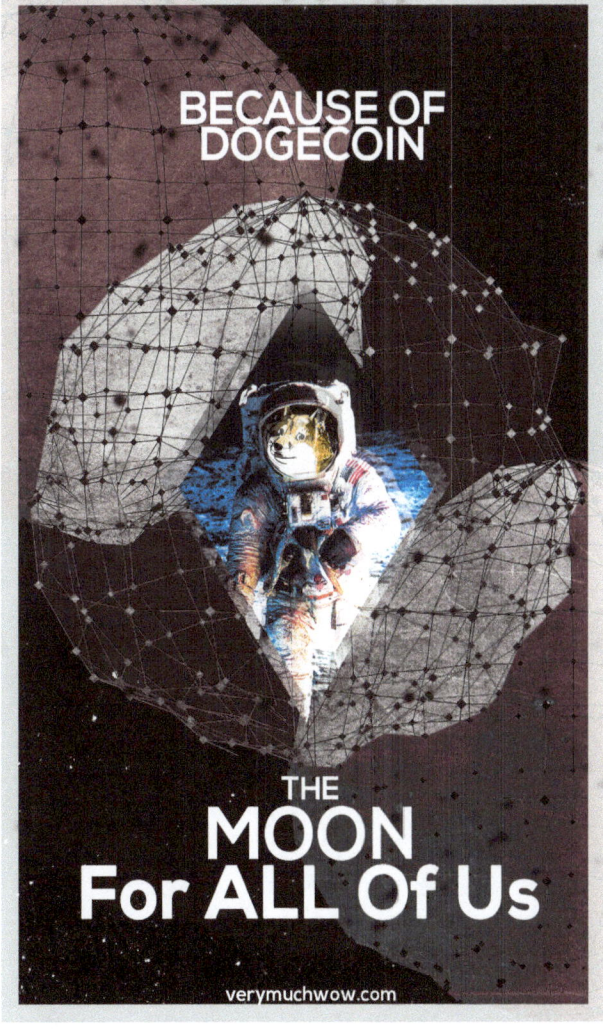

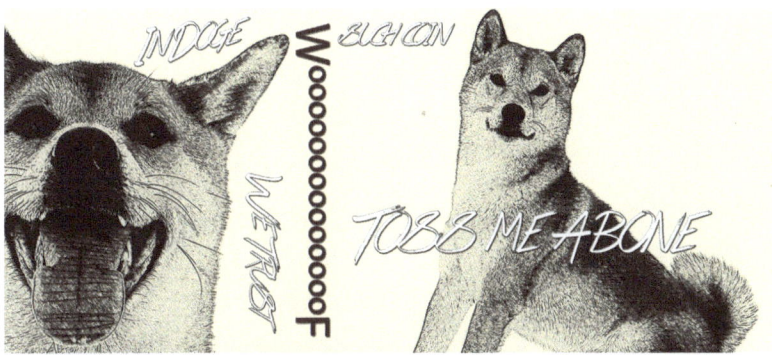

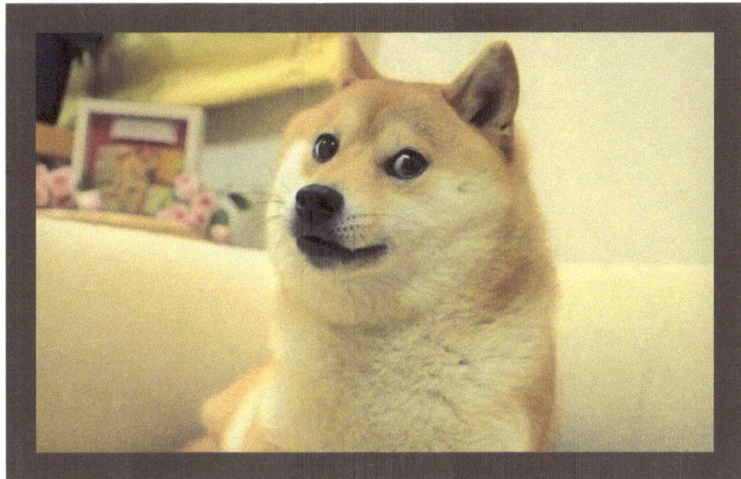